Made available through:

D1555293

INFANT NUTRITION
by Mark Percival D.C., N.D.

Published by: Health Coach® Systems International Inc.
e-mail www.healthcoach.com

Distributed by: IPS / Health Coach®
5525 North Union Blvd., Suite 203
Colorado Springs, Colorado
United States, 80918
1-800-348-1549

ISBN 0-9680104-0-7

Dedication

I dedicate this book to the love, innocence, truth and natural beauty that our precious daughter Aspen shares with us every magical moment which we spend with her. May we remain conscious enough to prevent our preoccupation with other lesser matters in life from dampening her natural spirit and enthusiasm for life.

I have prepared this guide in order to facilitate the healthy expression of each infant's unique spirit. It is an attempt to assist parents in the understanding and more effective management of the key nutritional factors which are so intimately linked to the expression of their infant's true potential.

Acknowledgments

Heartfelt thanks to: my loving partner and wife Cheri, whose patience and dedication helped to make this project possible, to my very special mother whose love, intuition and unselfishness continues to catalyse my spiritual growth, to my Health Coach colleagues and kindred spirits including Dr. Howard Levine, Dr. Timothy Brown and Dr. Charley Cropley for their inspiration and feedback, to my exceptional clinical team whose unfailing commitment to our patients and their work serves to free enough of my energies to tackle these special projects. Last, but certainly not least, to my patients, clients and friends who I have the great fortune to serve and learn from each day. They have most certainly facilitated my understanding of this challenging yet marvellous process which we have come to know as life. May we continue to learn together how to fully appreciate its many blessings and gifts.

Foreward

This booklet has been prepared for use within The Health Coach® System, a system of healthcare originated by Mark Percival D.C., N.D..

In this sytem, the primary role of health professionals is to guide and coach their patients and clients through healthier choices. Choices that assist them in understanding their body, what its signals mean and how specifically to care for it. The Health Coach® System also recognizes the primary role of the human mind and focuses appropriate emphasis on the emerging field of mind-body medicine. The functional application of this exciting and rapidly expanding field is explained and encouraged throughout Health Coach® System materials.

Everyday millions of people suffer needlessly and our healthcare budgets escalate as a direct result of both public and professional ignorance and ineffective approaches to healthcare. There is a clear need for better 'health coaching' and for more effective healthcare systems.

Dr. Percival's solution was to begin to develop a health education system which could meet, in large part, the demand for concise, straightforward explanations of the key areas which are essential to the recovery and the subsequent maintenance of our health.

His vision stems from his belief that healing is facilitated when individuals realize that they have the most significant resources, necessary to the healing of their lives, within them at all times. The creative intelligence which miraculously guides all forms of life is what allows for healing. This Vis Medicatrix Naturae or the Healing Power of Nature is the cornerstone of the Health Coach® System's educational programs. Mark's passion is to guide and coach people to understand and work with their body's marvelous self-healing and self-repair mechanisms.

As a colleague I have personally watched Mark develop The Health Coach® System from his own direct experience of more than a decade of busy clinical practice, while making positive changes in his own lifestyle habits, and presenting literally hundreds of seminars and workshops to both public and professionals.

Recognizing his limitations as just one individual, relative to the enormity of the task at hand, he has directed his focus toward developing The Health Coach® System and to empowering his fellow healthcare providers to participate in the ongoing development and delivery of this program to their respective communities. Acknowledging the dictum:

To hear is to forget.
To see is to remember,
To do is to understand.

Mark has incorporated audio, visual and participatory components into his program. Those healthcare providers who participate in the Health Coach® professional training program receive thorough instruction on the proper utilization of its educational materials.

As a healthcare provider and as a parent of five children I recognize that good infant nutrition is the foundation for health at later stages of life. It is a pleasure for me to see Mark producing a solid practical program of healthcare education and training for the benefit of all of us well-intentioned and busy parents.

Timothy W. Brown D.C., N.D.

Table of Contents

Infant Health

Whether you are presently planning to participate in the creation of a new life, or you are endeavouring to take superior care of one which has already been conceived, the information in this booklet has been written to facilitate your understanding of nutrition and lifestyle choices and their impact on your infant's health.

The essential components in your infant's health equation are:

$$\text{Infant Health} = \frac{\text{Inherited Potential (Genetics)}}{\text{Environmental Stressors (Distress)}}$$

Fig. 1

Inherited Potential: This represents the infant's collective genetic pool, determined by generations of ancestors on both parents' sides and is locked in at the moment of conception. Thus each infant's *potential* for health is pre-determined. This is not to be confused with each infant's *expression* of his/her health potential. Indeed, the infants' access to their inherited potential may be either facilitated or actually blocked by the environmental influences under which they are left to function.

Environmental Stressors: These represent all of the external influences which stress the infant. Some of which are within the parents' or guardians' control and some of which are not.

The environmental stressors may therefore be divided into two groups.

The Environmental Stressors

I. Those events and circumstances which are beyond the parents' or guardians' direct control. Thus, *choice is not involved.*

II. Those events and circumstances which are directly or indirectly within the parents' or guardians' control. Thus, *choice is involved.*

Fig. 2

It is the purpose of this text to facilitate your understanding of those factors which may adversely influence your infant's health and, wherever possible, to provide alternative choices, which when acted on, may benefit your infant. A healthy infant is a happy infant, and few sights in this world compare to the simple beauty and joy of such a being!

If our common goal is to improve your (current or your future) infant's health, what specifically may we do? The answer lies in the careful review and understanding of the simple equation of Fig. 1. The only variables in this equation on which we may focus beneficially are those *environmental influences with health significant impact where choice is involved.*

Let's proceed now to discuss these influences in order of their priority.

The Impact of Environment on Your Infant's Health

Factor #1 -Optimal Parental Health

This should not require explanation, but it has been my experience that it often does. In my 'coaching' of literally thousands of couples who have been either in the process of family planning, or already involved in the care of existing children, there have been relatively few who at least initially have fully appreciated the dramatic and the direct impact that **their health**, as parents, **has on their offspring**. Still fewer had accepted the responsibility which accompanies this reality and had taken control of these lifestyle choices, made moment to moment, day to day, week to week ... that have significant impact on their family's health.

The choice which you as parents must make every day, which has the most significant impact on your infant's health, directly and indirectly, is your general attitude toward life.

Attitudes of love, joy and genuine appreciation for your life and that of your child or children are the most fundamental building blocks for your children's health and the future quality of their lives.

Mental Attitude and Focus

Thoughts are 'things'. They instantaneously create energetic and neuro-chemical changes in your brain and throughout your entire body. They also impact your infant. Thus, positive resourceful thoughts can create an environment

We All Make
Daily Choices

within your body and home of love, appreciation, acceptance and respect. These positive 'states' favour the health and happiness of your family. On the other hand, unresourceful thoughts can, just as instantaneously produce feelings of anxiety, frustration, despair, rejection, guilt and fear. These negative states favour distress, dysfunction, pain and disease in yourself and in your infant.

For a more thorough discussion of this area refer to the Health Coach® System's booklet entitled <u>Teaming Up for a Healthier You, Understanding Healthcare and Stress Management</u>.

To summarize the discussion pertinent to this area, I stated that the most natural states for we human beings, both infants and adults alike, are those of joy, happiness and peace of mind. The key to the consistent access of these natural states is the absence of interference or distress. As discussed at length in the above mentioned booklet, distress results primarily from our focus and the resultant choices which we make moment to moment, and in the case of infants, the choices which parents make on their behalf.

For all parents who wish their infants and children the obvious joys and health benefits of a relatively stress-free environment, I urge you to consider that your attitude toward and around your infant and what you choose to feed them are the two major contributors to your infant's health and happiness or lack there of.

Let us all remember to thank our Creator for the unique ability which we humans have been granted. That is, the ability to choose our thoughts, our focus and thus our emotional state at any and all moments in time. Now let us continue to learn how to utilize this ability constructively, for the common good of our families, friends and our global environment.

NEGATIVE LESS RESOURCEFUL STATES	POSITIVE RESOURCEFUL STATES
FEAR	COURAGE
GUILT	PRIDE
ANGER	LOVE
DESPAIR	FAITH
SELF-DOUBT	SELF-CONFIDENCE
REJECTION	APPROVAL
DISAPPOINTMENT	GRATITUDE
APPREHENSION	ANTICIPATION
FRUSTRATION	FASCINATION
ETC.	ETC.

Note: The negative, less resourceful states or feelings, such as those listed above, serve an important purpose in your life. They serve to get your attention to interrupt your patterns of living. Once they have your attention however, there is little if any benefit to "hanging onto" them. Acknowledge them, give genuine thanks for their reminder and let them go!

For those of you who find this process difficult, get professional help and get it soon. Old, often lifelong patterns or habits are a challenge to change. There is no shame in accessing professional help with such challenges. Indeed, there is a great deal of relief and joy in doing so. Please... do this for yourself, for your spouse and for your children.

For those who find themselves struggling with the many challenges which are present in this area, I refer you to our remarkable Health Coach® video series and study guide titled "The Mind-Body Connection" and the following leading resources in this field of personal growth: Louise Hay, Deepak Chopra, Anthony Robbins, Wayne Dyer and Dennis Waitley. Their most recent books and audio-cassette programs are of exceptional value in learning to manage your mental/emotional resources more effectively. My favourites here are: Deepak's book Perfect Health and his tape series The Higher Self; Tony's book Awaken The Giant Within and his incredible 30-day audio cassette program Personal Power; Wayne's book Transformation, You Will See It When You Believe It and his tape series of the same title (you can't go wrong with any of his materials!); and Dennis's audio cassette album Seeds of Greatness. Your wisest investment is in developing yourself as a resource. What resources can serve more valuable than those which help you to manage your mental state more effectively?

I share great concern, for the parent and the physician alike, who fail to understand the directness of the connection here between the health state of an infant and the mental/emotional state of the infant's parents.

Exercising Your Options in Healthcare

How do you as a parent feel intuitively about many of today's *routine* practises in medicine? Such as the prescription of powerful drugs to suppress the symptoms of an infant's distress, in preference to taking the time to identify the actual cause and to effectively deal with it. I refer you to the Health Coach® Personalized Education

Program articles (P.E.P. Steps) titled "Health vs. Disease" and "Understanding the Actions of Drugs in Relation to Natural Law", located in your P.E.P. Binder (should you have one) or available from your participating Health Coach® center.

This common practice of prescribing drugs for infant signs and symptoms is perhaps best exemplified by the recent statistics on the use of prescription drugs in pediatric care. These reports reveal an average number of prescriptions for children, by the ripe old age of five, to range from fifteen to fifty! That is an average of from three to ten per year, per infant.

Does this indeed represent the picture of a progressive healthcare system which effectively deals with the key health issues of our time in a resourceful fashion? Why then does the Western medical establishment continue to publicize such a rosy picture? One of increased well-being and quality of life, yet allergies, upper respiratory conditions, asthma, skin conditions, digestive problems, diabetes, arthritises, circulatory diseases, cancers and a wide array of unexplained immune disorders continue to increase all around us! Is this an honest case of misdirected focus and genuine ignorance on behalf of our medical and legislative establishments?

Condemnation in the absence of thorough investigation is thought by many to represent the height of ignorance. Our medical establishment is certainly guilty of this in the area of natural healthcare. A more balanced and functional model for a healthcare system must be designed. By 'balanced' and 'functional' I refer to a system which recognizes the adage "An ounce of prevention is worth a pound of cure" to be a truism. In response, this system would focus on the areas of *health promotion* and *disease prevention* and it would do so with a passion parallel to that which is applied to disease management in our current system. This system would not be profit driven, it would be saving driven. The portion of our healthcare dollars spent on disease management, in preference to *health promotion* and *disease prevention*, in our current system, runs at approximately ninety-nine percent! This is astonishing as one reviews study after study that confirms the incredible benefits of preventive lifestyle approaches in contrast to the gross limitations of the current "just fix it when it's broke" model of healthcare.

For those interested in the details of an alternative approach to our healthcare challenges, I refer you to our Health Coach® audio program titled "Principle-Centered Living, Leadership and Healthcare". For those of you who wish to decrease your dependence on our disease-care system (which in turn will serve to relieve some of the pressure on it and thus allow for a broader focus in the future) there is a great deal which you can do right now by simply acting on the information within these pages.

We began by discussing the role which our mental and emotional habits play in our health and that of our infants and children, as they are of paramount importance, now let us proceed to the other factors or lifestyle choices which are also pertinent to your infant's health.

Factor #2 - Nurture of Nature

Nourishment

Once again, the most important 'nourishment' for all infants is the unconditional love and acceptance of their parents and care providers. Second only to these considerations are the need for: clean air, pure water and those high quality foods and beverages which are *readily digestible* to an infant's unique little tummy!

The Breath of Life

The nutrient which is most crucial to human life and that indeed none of us can function without, for even a few minutes, is oxygen. The prenatal infant is entirely dependent on its mother and the efficiency of her respiratory and circulatory systems for this life sustaining nutrient throughout its crucial first nine months of development. The efficiency of the mother's respiratory and circulatory systems are directly influenced, once again, by her lifestyle habits. The key considerations here are: exercise habits, rest and nutrition habits and of course the quality of the air which Mom breathes day in and day out. (We don't need to discuss the choking asphyxiation of carbon monoxide from cigarette smoke on the helpless fetus here do we?)

The following comes as a surprise to many, **but the quality of the air in most people's homes is many times more toxic than that outside of their homes, even in urban and inner city settings. Studies have found air contamination levels to be as much as seventy times higher indoors than outdoors!**

Yes parents, **you can effectively create a superior environment indoors.** This is an important step in the effective prevention and/or management of any respiratory conditions in your household. These include: runny noses, sinusitis, bronchitis, asthma, allergies and recurrent cold signs and symptoms. But please don't wait for any of these conditions to manifest before you act on the challenge of improving air quality in your home, office or recreational dwellings. Air quality factors into all of our health equations sooner or later.

Solutions to this challenge begin with the use of: non-toxic, biodegradable household cleaning products, non-toxic paints, superior vacuum and air filtration/ventilation systems, cleaner heat sources and abstinence from such polluting habits as smoking and the use of chemicals (of any kind) indoors.

Keep in mind that our lungs not only function to deliver oxygen to every cell, tissue and organ system in our body, they also are our most vital detoxification organ! That's right, our lungs eliminate approximately 75% of total body wastes, in the form of gases, day after day after day. The two tablespoons of dirt and dust with which the average respiratory system must cope each day, can be significantly reduced by acting on the aforementioned steps to improved air quality. Be certain to discuss the specifics of these steps with your participating Health Coach® center (For the Health Coach® center nearest you, call 1-519-662-2520) and a qualified specialist in air purification.

Optimal Nutrition: "Quality vs. Quantity"

Over the past four decades Western industrialized nations have witnessed relative affluence. We have also led more sedentary lifestyles, made possible through a host of technological advances and the associated urbanization of much of our society. During these 'good times', food quantity has received much attention, while food quality has received little. Corporate giants race against one another in pursuit of the next 'technological advance' which may give them an edge in the marketplace and their primary focus remains quantity. The sales pitch heard throughout our society continues "with our product you get more for less". What a concept! The reality however is more aptly stated, "with our product you get *more of less*!"

What are the real costs to both the individual and our society of this quantitative focus? Even our agricultural system, the very source of the fuel which sustains our marvelous human physiology, has made numerous compromises with respect to quality, in favour of quantity. Yet thousands of tons of food sit spoiling every day while decisions about distribution are made, based primarily on the *quantity of dollars* involved. At the same time, petrochemical interests continue to successfully convince legislators, farmers and even the public, that lacing our soils and foodstuffs with relatively toxic synthetic petrochemical by-products is essential for the maintenance of our quantity-based ($) food production system.

Enter the food manufacturing and processing industry, where it is commonplace to take the already nutrient deficient agricultural products and *process* them in order to extend shelf life or to capitalize on consumer ignorance and susceptibility to 'slick' marketing strategies. Such processing more often than not, results in the addition of still more potentially toxic petrochemical by-products to our foodstuffs. These newly packaged, adulterated versions of nature's bounty, are then shipped to retail food outlets, where all to often point-of-purchase mis- and dys- information further serves to foil even the more wary consumers in their attempt to make the best choices with respect to their health.

Fortunately, a growing number of researchers and progressive health professionals are striving to understand the full impact of the resulting nutrient-depleted, chemically altered diets on human health. This same group is also seeking alternative methods and solutions to the growing challenges presented by the demise of the North American diet. Meanwhile, the petrochemical industry continues to expand its horizons in yet another area: the exceptionally lucrative, legal drug market, where yet another series of synthetic and often highly toxic petrochemical by-products are being manufactured for human consumption in the form of both prescription and non-prescription drugs. The irony in this scenario is that the need for many of these drugs, has been in large part created and continues to be supported by the aforementioned manipulation of our foods and the associated reduction in the quality of our diets. (The more sedentary lifestyles which modern technology has afforded us must be considered here as well.)

Those readers who may be thinking... *"But heretics like Dr. Percival would have people starving... and for what?"...* had better find a seat now as I share some harsh realities with you. People are starving right now. In fact, some 60,000,000 people will starve this year. Another child has starved in the time it has taken for you to read this sentence, yes, one child every two seconds, *40,000 everyday.* The human population of the United States and Canada combined is 265,000,000. The number of human beings that could be fed by the grains and soybeans eaten by American and Canadian livestock alone is 1,300,000,000 almost five times our total population.

In addition:

- The percentage of proteins wasted when cycling grain through livestock is 90%.
- The percentage of carbohydrate wasted when cycling grain through livestock is greater than 90%.
- The percentage of fiber wasted when cycling grain through livestock is 100%.
- Pounds of potatoes that can be grown on one acre of land is approximately 20,000.
- Pounds of beef that can be produced on one acre of land is approximately 165.
- Pounds of grain and soybeans needed to produce one pound of feedlot beef is approximately 16.*

Need I continue... perhaps, but this is not the place. Suffice it to say that our society's focus on the quantity of animal products that it produces is a $dollar issue, not a need-based or quality of life issue. Our culture and indeed our global society would be much better for a shift in focus, back to the

---

* *J. Robbins - "Diet For A New America"*

nutritional qualities of our agricultural products and food supplies, in preference to our current quantitative focus. With wise management, we have ample resources to feed our world's population sufficiently, without compromising the quality of our food supplies. There is simply no justification (outside of $dollar) for the unnatural and often inhumane treatment of farm (or any other) animals.

For those interested in developing a better understanding of the impact that their nutrition and lifestyle choices have on our global society, you may contact:

> Earthsave   (408) 423-4069
> 706 Fredrick Street
> Santa Cruz, CA
> 95062-2205

I would like to add that I am not *against* the consumption of clean, minimally processed animal products, nor am I on a campaign to convert the reader to vegetarianism. I am however *for* **informed consumption**. It is time that you the consumer be empowered to think for yourself, in preference to somewhat naively following the carefully placed propaganda of powerful marketing boards or self-interest groups. In order to do so effectively, you need accurate information, shared with compassion and concern, and not tainted for power and profit. On careful review of the facts and after clearing away the cobwebs of hearsay, the conscientious consumers find themselves choosing a relatively chemical-free, higher quality, less processed and *usually* more plant based diet, while feeling remarkably better for it.

Let it suffice at this point to say that the information in this text will focus on **quality** in preference to quantity, and **ecology** in preference to just economy. Indeed, if one attends to quality properly, quantity usually looks after itself. You will find that this information is designed to help you to make important qualitative distinctions, yet you will find few references to quantities of the foods discussed. Trust your instincts and those of your infant here, along with the specific feedback of your participating Health Coach® center.

Numerous epidemiological studies now support the aforementioned discussion, as does simple common sense. By far, the most important experience for this author was to **first make the qualitative changes** in his own diet **and** to thus **observe the impact** on his own health. He has since personally witnessed dramatic changes in the health of thousands of clients as the direct result of their making more informed dietary choices.

To coin an old phrase "The proof is in the pudding", you have only to implement and then experience for yourself the merits of an improved diet. What have you to lose? Please remember that in your quest for improved health through better nutrition, every one of us is as unique chemically as we are physically. This fact necessitates a strategy which serves to identify the specific foods, nutrients and nutrition principles which best suit each individual's specific physiology. The guidelines to assist you in accomplishing this for your infant are present in this text, however the guidelines for you and the rest of your 'non-infant' family can be found in our Health Coach® publication Functional Dietetics, The Core of Health Integration and our video series The Diet-Health Connection. Please note, that this is a process which often requires the kind of corrective and directive feedback that only a properly qualified nutrition-oriented healthcare professional such as a Health Coach® participant, can provide effectively. (Refer to Fig.3 on page 18) Accordingly, you the reader are urged to seek out the advice of such a professional and keep to the consultation schedule which they advise. Follow his/her instructions implicitly, keep careful notes on your diet and that of your infant and record all the signs and symptoms as directed. The key to your success with your program depends to a great extent on your ability to seek out and then effectively communicate with your "health coach". So please, be sure to do so wherever possible.

Healthcare, especially with respect to infants who for obvious reasons cannot communicate well, is a complicated challenge. A challenge with little to no room for error. Please readers, do not take unnecessary chances with your infant's health! Always seek competent advice promptly and if your child is not responding and his/her distress continues, get back to your health professional without delay. If still not satisfied, get another opinion. If opinions conflict, **use your common sense, listen to your instincts and those of the doctor who shows the most genuine concern for the well-being of you and your infant.**

Natural is not always better than synthetic, nor is non-invasive always better than invasive. There are those situations where drugs and/or other relatively invasive procedures are indicated. We can be genuinely grateful for their availability and the diligence and skill of the doctors and support personnel who provide these services. They most certainly have their place in disease management, where the danger or threat posed by the disease condition is greater than that posed by the drug or surgical procedure and there is no equally effective, less invasive method available.

It continues to be this author's experience however, that such situations are fewer and farther between, for those who are willing to accept the responsibility for their health and that of their family. This is best accomplished through a proactive approach to both health promotion and disease prevention. I would also like to add that I am not against the petrochemical industry, indeed I acknowledge and enjoy the comforts of their efforts in a number of areas, nor am I against mainstream (allopathic) medicine. I am simply in support of the search for truths, in the relative absence of self-serving, economically driven or profit-centered biases. I am for the individual's right to choice in healthcare. Monopolistic policies have little place in healthcare, yet they continue to surround and to choke our current system (and many who are dependent upon it).

Eventually, we will have a cooperative healthcare system, which encourages complimentary care and involves an array of conscientious health disciplines working in concert for the common good of the client, the community and the system as a whole.

You can play a significant role in helping to shift the emphasis in our current system, from that of disease to that of health, by simply:

- studying the following materials carefully
- following the guidance and instructions of a properly qualified health professional
- observing first hand the impact on your infant's state of health
- then sharing what you have learned with others in your community, including the legislators and policy makers.
- sharing your new knowledge and experience with other health professionals who may then learn through your experience.

For those readers who are interested in an overview of what the components of such a *health-based system* might include, refer to the Health Coach® publication <u>Teaming Up For A Healthier You</u>.

Figure 3

<u>Current Nutritional Considerations</u>

Biochemical Individuality
Each individual is as unique biochemically as he/she is physically. Thus biochemical/nutritional needs vary considerably among our population.

Genetotrophic Factors: Nutrient requirements are linked to genetic make up and thus vary widely from person to person. Specific nutrient requirements, to provide for optimal function, may vary as much as tenfold between individuals.

Lifestyle: Each person's lifestyle also directly impacts his/her need for specific nutrients. Considerations here include:

- Exercise Levels
- Food & Beverage Choices
- Refined Carbohydrate Intake
- Food Additive Consumption
- Air and Water Quality
- Chemical Adulteration of Food
- Gastrointestinal Absorption Characteristics
- Bioenergetic Patterns *

- Alcohol Intake
- Drug Use/Abuse
- Overconsumption

* Bioenergetic (human energy) patterns not only differ from person to person, but they are dynamic in nature and continuously shift within each individual. Such 'energy shifts' may indeed influence how we function on the biochemical level, therefore shifting our metabolism, how we utilize specific nutrients and thus varying our micronutrient needs from time to time .

Environmental Pollution: Exposure to air, water, food, household and occupational contaminants all influence one's need for the various antioxidant nutrients which help to neutralize these toxins in the body.

Food Processing Techniques: Food processing has led to significant reductions in the much needed fibre, essential oil and antioxidant content of foods.

Intensive Agricultural Techniques:
- soil nutrient depletion
- crop hybridization

Such practices have unfortunately resulted in nutrient depleted soil and the development of crop hybrids which do not always meet consumer nutrient needs as well as they meet food producers' economic needs.

Food Cosmetic Treatment: Consumers today must also cope with a broad array of colourings, waxes and disinfectants, the long-term effects of which, only time may tell.

Food Harvesting, Storage & Transportation: Many factors come to play in this complex area, with one of the unfortunate results often being compromised food nutrient value.

Health Conditions: A wide variety of health conditions from pregnancy, lactation, and menopause, to various infectious or degenerative disease states, to traumatic or toxic conditions, to shifts in bioenergetic (mental-emotional-physiological) patterns significantly impact one's need for specific nutrients.

The previously discussed factors combine to make obsolescent the belief that all one must do to obtain optimal nutrition is to eat a 'balanced diet'. Indeed, optimal nutrition does begin with a whole-food, properly varied diet, but it no longer ends there. Optimization of the micronutrients (trace elements and antioxidants especially) more often than not requires specific supplementation, on the advice of a properly qualified, nutrition-oriented healthcare professional, such as those found at participating Health Coach® centers. This follows the thorough evaluation of each individual's unique nutritional requirements, considering all of the aforementioned factors. Be certain to ask your participating Health Coach® (should you have one already) about the health appraisal questionnaires, specialized lab tests and nutrition-oriented physical exam designed specifically for this purpose. All readers are encouraged to seek out such a properly qualified nutrition-oriented health professional for a personal evaluation of their more unique nutrient needs. For the clinics participating in the Health Coach® System nearest you call 519-662-2520.

For a more general yet comprehensive overview of the key nutrient requirements which most people in our Western culture share please refer to our audio program "Body by Design, Health by Choice" tape 6, side B and the related section in its study guide titled "Resolving Sub-Optimal Levels of Key Nutrients".

Most parents reviewing the last three pages will undoubtedly note that their nutrient needs have not been adequately assessed, let alone met. Further, your nutritional status as parents, pre-conception in both your case and post-conception in mom's case, as well as throughout her pregnancy and lactation has had (or will have) a direct impact on your infant's requirements for various nutrients. In other words, sub-optimally nourished parents give birth to sub-optimally nourished infants. As you may already be aware, such sub-optimal nutritional status is the rule today, not the exception. Fortunately, there is much you can do to correct this scenario both before and after the fact.

Setting the Stage for Health

Congratulations! It's a baby girl/boy! ...now what??!!

Remember at all times, first and foremost, to love and adore your infant, accept them exactly as and how they are, unconditionally. Second, only to the above, provide them with as pollution-free an environment as possible and ... oh yes, feed them right! Would you like some specific direction in the area of infant nutrition? There seem to be so many experts around all of a sudden, don't there!

Fortunately, there is one expert that you can always count on, Mother Nature; and what does she provide for all infants ... that's right, breast milk. From a healthy mother of course, one who has read and applies the principles found within our guidebook <u>Functional Dietetics, The Core of Health Integration</u>. It might have been some authors preference to combine these two publications, for the convenience of some readers. However, the sheer volume of the resultant publication would have intimidated all but the most studious of parents among us and might thus have served to discourage many from addressing even the simplest of these challenges.

Breast-Feeding

The young of all mammals, humans included, are best nourished by the fresh whole raw milk produced from their own species. This is precisely why females are equipped with milk-producing glands. In the past five decades, far too many well-intentioned mothers have prematurely replaced breast milk with an unfounded reliance on the commercial food industry.

- In the early 1900's, approximately 99% of infants were breast-fed. Baby bottles were unheard of.
- In the mid-fifties, studies showed less than 40% of infants were breast-fed.
- As of the late sixties, only 20% of infants were breast-fed.

Several factors account for this disturbing trend. First, the rapid onset of industrialization and urbanization resulted in many mothers working outside of the home. Second, the women's liberation movement had an effect by those advocates who depict breast-feeding as confining and even demeaning. Additionally, the social pressures on new mothers to bottle-feed their babies, as the result of the massive advertising campaigns by the manufacturers of these commercial formulas. Millions of dollars are spent annually by these manufacturers in order to convince both mothers and their physicians that the highly processed, somewhat artificial, baby food compounds are acceptable substitutes for breast milk in some instances. In fairness to the commercial formula industry however, it must be pointed out that advertising policies in this area are changing, with some manufacturers even including literature in support of breast-feeding and its superiority in their literature. For this I applaud them. At the core of the above factors is **the absence of adequate training in the field of nutrition, especially infant nutrition, for the vast majority of today's healthcare professionals.**

As the limitations of the synthetic, chemicalized trend, to which so many of our food manufacturers have resorted, become more apparent, many women are returning to breast-feeding. These parents in turn discover that breast-feeding results in healthier, happier babies for the following reasons:

- Breast milk introduces and encourages the growth of the desirable beneficial bacteria in the infant's digestive tract. Formulas on the other hand are: sterilized, devoid of these beneficial bacteria, high in refined carbohydrates, more difficult to digest and thus may even favour the growth of less desirable, putrefactive and fermentative bacteria, yeast and fungal organisms. (As evidenced by the odour of their excrement!)

- Breast-fed babies are less likely to develop allergies later in life, especially to foods. Both formulas and the early introduction of pablums and other solid foods prompt allergies to develop.

- Breast-fed babies are less prone to skin disorders and eczemas.

- Breast-feeding encourages good facial and dental development. Bottle-fed babies are more prone to poorly developed facial structures, palates and dental arches.

- Breast-fed babies have increased resistance to infection due to the immune-enhancing factors in their mother's milk.

- Breast-fed babies have fewer digestive upsets and generally sleep better because they digest breast milk better than formulas. (Provided that their mothers are on proper diets of course.)

If these points are not enough, consider that mothers who breast-feed have a lower incidence of breast cancer than women who do not, breast milk is more convenient on many occasions and the act of holding the child to her breast has been shown to enhance the bonding process between mother and child and to help to build a more loving, secure relationship. Don't all infants deserve such a start?

To those mothers who feel that breast-feeding just is not for them, we will be discussing your best available alternatives later in this text. I appeal to these mothers however to consider all of the aspects involved here and not just those that support a largely emotional decision which you may regret later. There is no right or wrong here, but there is good, better and best and I am of the opinion that what is best for your newborn infant will in the final analysis, prove to be best for you as a mother. If you will take a few moments to reflect on your significant accomplishments of the past, haven't they all involved going beyond your comfort zone, in pursuit of worthwhile goals? Do you recall how you felt about going beyond your comfort level at the time? How did you feel about your decision after the fact? Well, here is another such opportunity for you to learn and to grow in a positive direction. The final decision of course must rest with you, the infant's mother, as your peace of mind is as essential to your infant's health as any nutritional factor. Make the decision which you understand is best and proceed confidently from that point. There are no mistakes when raising children out of love and appreciation, only lessons. Regret and guilt have no constructive place in a functional home. Learn to listen to and trust your deepest intuition, it will seldom, if ever, mislead you.

Infant Digestion

Understanding Your Infant's Limitations

At birth, your infant's digestive system is still developing and is not yet ready to carry out the complex tasks of masticating (liquefying) and digesting (breaking down) foods. Your infant, of course, has no teeth yet and the salivary secretions necessary for proper starch breakdown are still insufficient. **The salivary secretions responsible for initiating starch breakdown are not present in significant concentrations until around the time the first teeth appear** (commonly five to six months of age). This is often accompanied by a noticeable increase in saliva and drooling.

The next step in the breakdown of more complex starches occurs in the small intestine and involves an enzyme called pancreatic amylase. There are widely respected experts in pediatric gastro-enterology, who assert that this essential enzyme does not appear until close to eighteen months of age and certainly not before twelve months. Yet the first foods that many well-intentioned but unfortunately ill-advised health professionals suggest introducing, are pablum or cereal, made from grains which are complex carbohydrates.

Feeding infants foods which they cannot digest properly merely leads to the decomposition of these foods in their intestines and the associated challenges which result. These include the most common infant complaints of today, namely: colic, irritability, insomnia, constipation or diarrhea, bloating and gas, skin rashes and eczemas, recurrent upper respiratory infections, allergies and asthma. This is not to say that the subsequent treatment of the above conditions stops with diet modification, but appropriate treatment must certainly include it. Participating Health Coach® centers will understand the relationship here, but the majority of participants in our healthcare delivery system may not, as their training has emphasized and focused on other aspects of healthcare.

It is however difficult to understand those healthcare providers who vehemently deny any possible connection between what an infant (or anyone else for that matter) ingests and how they function. More puzzling still, is why many of these individuals have neglected to take it upon themselves to properly investigate the interplay between food and health, an obvious connection for even the less schooled (and less biased) lay person.

How do I profess to know what others have researched clinically and what they have not? It is quite simple. *To do is to understand.* All who do *reasonable* clinical research here, begin to understand the true relevance of nutrition's role in health and disease, thus dissolving any opposition on their part. I *understand,* as do participating Health Coach® centers, because this is the area with which we work, day after day, client after client, infant after infant, and we see the remarkable transitions in health which result. This is in the absence of the suppressing "cover up" effects of any drugs, which so readily mask the true state of an infant's or client's health. Who should you, the reader, believe? How about your own direct experience from the results which you achieve by following a sensible program. The choice of programs is yours. The Health Coach® System is committed to seeing that you indeed get a choice. A choice that can do no harm when followed as coached and has the potential for a great deal of good, both personally and ultimately globally.

The argument that children must be fed solid foods to enhance their growth and development is simply not supported by any valid evidence or properly controlled studies. To quote a recognized authority in the field of infant nutrition, Dr. L.F. Hill from the Committee on Nutrition of the American Academy of Pediatrics on The Feeding of Solid Foods to Infants, "the early introduction of solid foods into the infant diet is the result of empiricism and competition, not of sound nutritional principles. It is attended by certain dangers, which are not compensated for by any discernible advantages."

An infant's gastrointestinal tract is designed to maximize digestion and absorption of the constituents of human breast milk. These include: proteins, carbohydrates (beta-lactose), fats/oils, minerals, vitamins, enzymes and water.

The newborn's stomach secretions contain pepsin and hydrochloric acid, both of which are effective protein and mineral digestants. In the baby's pancreatic secretions, there are the protein and fat digesting enzymes, trypsin and steapsin respectively. It appears that the carbohydrate which newborns are best equipped to digest is the milk sugar, lactose. Lactose is broken down with the aid of the enzyme lactase, which is present in infants' small intestines. The above enzymes are sufficient to digest the constituents of human breast milk effectively, while the relatively permeable walls of the infant's small intestine ensure maximum absorption.

What happens when foods other than breast milk are introduced too early? The enhanced absorption characteristics of an infant's small intestine (in comparison to that of an older child or adult) and the limited digestive capacity, combine to allow for increased uptake, from the intestine into the blood, of incompletely digested proteins or *antigens*. The infant's immune system subsequently identifies these antigens as foreign, non-utilizable and potentially harmful and attempts to remove them from the blood by forming antibodies. Antibodies are substances produced by our body's immune system which facilitate the elimination of antigens (foreign substances) which find their way into our blood and tissues.

The human body has been created with a marvellous array of protective barriers and mechanisms which generally serve to prevent foreign substances from entering it and interfering with its function. These include our skin and the mucous membranes which line our respiratory and gastrointestinal systems. These organs, our *outer* and *inner* skins, are where all direct contact, of a physical nature, occurs daily with the external environment. There is a direct relationship between the state of our health and the integrity of these two protective organs. They indeed are where our internal environment interfaces with our external environment. They function to keep what must remain inside in and what must remain outside out, while they constantly allow for a selective exchange of both nutrients and wastes; as required in the maintenance of the intricate balance necessary for our healthy function.

In our discussion of the infant's gastrointestinal system, it is important to note that **not only does it differ from that of a more mature gut with respect to its digestive secretions, but it also differs with respect to the function of the mucous membranes which line it.** This is particularly true in the small intestine where the barrier function has been compromised in order to enhance the absorption function. In other words, **the infant's small intestine, especially during the first nine months of life, serves to absorb its contents (the foods ingested) more rapidly and with less discretion than that of the adult gut.** This means that foods which have not been reduced by the available digestive enzymes, to their basic nutrient components, are more likely to find their way into the infant's circulation and to then trigger antibody formation. These antibodies then remain in circulation for many years and perhaps even a lifetime. (see Fig. 4 on page 31)

Subsequently in the future, when the same foods that originally triggered the antibody formation are eaten, the body will respond via its immunological defence system. The immune system releases such powerful pro-inflammatory substances as histamines and leukotrienes, often provoking any of a myriad of symptoms, which health scientists are only just recently linking to these *food reactions*. Once again, these can include many of the common infant and childhood health disorders such as: colic, abdominal gas and bloating, constipation, diarrhea, skin rashes and eczema, recurrent upper respiratory infections, asthma, tonsillitis, ear infections, mood swings, irritability and behavioural problems.

Virtually any food fed to an infant before the age of six months may contribute to these food reactions or allergies. The later a food is introduced to your infant, the more mature their gastrointestinal system and the less likely that they will react in this fashion. Is it any wonder that the foods commonly fed to infants in these early months are the most common allergens found in the adolescent and adult population? These include cow's milk and milk products, wheat, corn, citrus fruits, eggs, yeast and soy products. You may note that this list reads much like the list of ingredients found in most infant formulas.

Complicating the scenario further is the fact that the early introduction of one food, for example cow's milk, may trigger intolerance to other foods introduced at a later date, such as corn or wheat. This is due to the food antigen's inflammatory effect on the gut membranes and the subsequent further increase in their permeability. This phenomenon referred to as the 'leaky gut' syndrome has been linked to the pan-allergic conditions which are becoming increasingly common especially in our children. These are the tragic cases where the child has become hyper-sensitive to so many foods and substances, that their life becomes a constant juggling act, as parent and child scramble to minimize exposure to any and all, now toxic antigens. Fortunately there are solutions to these challenges, where, under the guidance of a skilled Health Coach® participant, the child's 'leaky gut' is restored, normalizing its barrier and absorption functions while a more resourceful dietary plan is established.

Digestion, Gut Permeability, Food Allergy and Bowel Toxicity

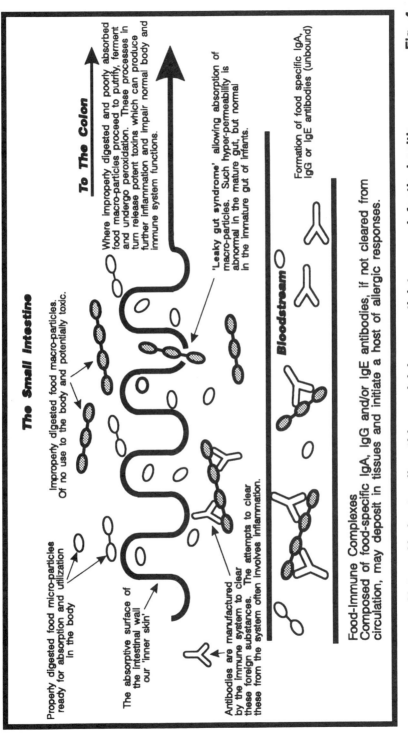

The Small Intestine

Properly digested food micro-particles ready for absorption and utilization in the body

Improperly digested food macro-particles. Of no use to the body and potentially toxic.

The absorptive surface of the intestinal wall our 'inner skin'

Antibodies are manufactured by the immune system to clear these foreign substances. The attempts to clear these from the system often involves inflammation.

To The Colon

Where improperly digested and poorly absorbed food macro-particles proceed to putrify, ferment and undergo peroxidation. These processes in turn release potent toxins which can produce further inflammation and impair normal body and immune system functions.

'Leaky gut syndrome' allowing absorption of macro-particles. Such hyper-permeability is abnormal in the mature gut, but normal in the immature gut of infants.

Bloodstream

Formation of food specific IgA, IgG or IgE antibodies (unbound)

Food-Immune Complexes
Composed of food-specific IgA, IgG and/or IgE antibodies, if not cleared from circulation, may deposit in tissues and initiate a host of allergic responses.

Note: Understanding this model is essential to your infant's health. Please review it with your Health Coach™.

Fig. 4

The Sacred Cow..... Dispelled

Contrary to what most of us have been taught, cow's milk, which appears so similar to breast milk, is not the most appropriate food, especially for an infant in its first year of life. In fact, cow's milk may be more of a problem than a solution when it comes to infant nutrition. Despite the similarities in appearance between breast milk and cow's milk, they are actually quite different in their nutritional composition.

The Comparison (Momma to Moo-moo)

Protein:

Cow's milk contains almost three times as much protein as breast milk. Infants can seldom manage the digestive burden this places on the protein-splitting enzymes of their stomach and pancreas. This may lead to the incomplete breakdown of these dairy products. When any protein molecules are not properly broken down in the gut, two scenarios may develop. One scenario has the undigested portion of the protein passing through the small intestine intact and decomposing lower in the intestinal tract, thereby producing toxic putrefactive by-products, more recognizable as bloating, foul smelling stools and often colic. The other scenario involves the absorption of a significant portion of the incompletely digested proteins into the bloodstream. This triggers an immune response designed to clear the blood of these 'foreign' proteins. This immune response often involves antibody formation, specific to the invading proteins and setting the stage for future allergic reactions. Neither of these scenarios are desirable and both can be avoided by the conscientious parent.

Please consider that cow's milk is tailored to double a calf's weight in fifty days. On the other hand, a human infant's weight doubles in two to three times that period. Not only is there a difference in protein quantity, but also in its quality. The protein in cow's milk is approximately 85% casein and 15% whey. In human milk, casein constitutes only 40% and whey constitutes 60%. Whey proteins are water soluble and much easier to digest than casein protein. Some researchers claim that excess casein tends to form difficult-to-digest curds in the human stomach.

The calf on the other hand, for which nature has designed cow's milk, has four stomachs which contain powerful, highly specialized digestive bacteria and an abundance of the casein-digesting enzyme, rennin. Could the above factors combine to explain *some* of the colic, bowel and immune problems seen in so many of our little ones consuming cow's milk these days?

Amino acids are the building blocks of proteins. The amino acid composition of human milk differs considerably from that of cow's milk. Human milk is higher in cysteine, an important sulfur-containing amino acid. This may account for infants' superior assimilation of human milk proteins (by as much as 100%) over that of cow's milk. Cysteine is also a key component in an important detoxification pathway. As such, it is vital to the protection of the infant's cells and tissues from the damaging effects of foreign chemicals and potentially toxic metabolic waste products.

Fats and Fatty Acid Composition:

Fatty acids are to fats what amino acids are to proteins. Fatty acids are the building blocks of fats. The differences here between human and cow's milk are significant as well. According to the World Health Organization, human milk contains an average of 4.4% milk fat. Recent studies demonstrate a wide variation in the actual composition of these fats depending on the mother's diet. On average, human milk fat contains approximately 8% of the highly beneficial omega-6 essential fatty acid, linoleic acid. It also contains varying amounts of gamalinolenic acid (GLA) and dihomogamalinolenic acid (DGLA), two equally important precursors of the PGI series of prostaglandins. These prostaglandins are valuable hormone-like substances which play many roles, not the least of which are those involved in the protective role against inflammation and degenerative diseases. None of these highly labile (unstable) fatty acids are present, in significant quantities, in cow's milk or any other dairy products, especially after processing.

It is also important to note that studies comparing the relative percentages of these essential fatty acids in people on different diets, have shown that much higher levels of these oils are present in the milk of mothers following a more plant-based diet. This group also displayed a much lower percentage of the sticky and potentially toxic saturated fats in their milk. Mothers consuming more plant-based diets have also been found to have far less pesticide residues in their breast milk than those on more meat-based diets. Thus confirming what many food scientists have been claiming for years, that eating from lower on the food chain can minimize the concentration of such toxic chemicals in our body tissues and fluids. Cow's milk averages about 3.5% fat, not dissimilar to that of human milk. However its fatty acid profile is considerably different. Most importantly, cow's milk contains very little of the valuable essential fatty acids and is considerably higher in the sticky and frequently more toxic saturated fatty acids.

Lower levels of essential fatty acids and higher levels of the sticky saturated fats in one's diet have been linked to the development of a long list of degenerative diseases which include liver-gallbladder disease, cardiovascular disease and even some types of cancers. We are beginning to understand these as diseases which get their start very early in our development. Early signs often related to deficiency of the essential fatty acids are: dry skin, eczema, chronic diaper rash, digestive upset, diarrhea, excessive thirst and lowered resistance to infection.

Note: An important supplement, which many infants require is the addition of these essential fatty acids. This is especially true for those infants who are not being breast fed or whose mother is on a high animal protein diet. Be sure to consult your Health Coach® participant (where possible) about this important topic, as you will need coaching here with respect to the quality and quantity of any supplements you are considering. For those readers without access to a participating Health Coach® professional, I refer you to our text Functional Dietetics section on "Fats and Oils", and Part 4 of our Diet-Health Connection video education series also titled "Fats and Oils". Meanwhile, if you skip ahead to page 66, 69 and 70 of this text you'll gain a better understanding of some of the important distinctions to be made around what oils to include in your infant's diet.

Carbohydrates:

Human milk contains approximately twice the milk sugar (lactose), than that of cow's milk. Some researchers state that there are subtle yet significant differences between the lactose in human breast milk and that of cows. Human breast milk they say contains a form of lactose known as beta-lactose, while cow's milk contains alpha-lactose. The nature of the beta-lactose in mother's milk selectively favours the growth of specialized strains of the beneficial bacteria lactobacilus acidophilius and bifida bacteria. These beneficial microorganisms: produce enzymes which help to break down carbohydrates, inhibit the growth of pathogens and yeasts in the gut, contribute to the formation of naturally-occurring antibiotics and anti-carcinogens, and even produce some of the B-complex vitamins.

Many formula-fed infants who do not get the opportunity to receive the important inoculation of these beneficial bacteria into their digestive tract via breast-feeding (their only significant source), can go on to become lactose intolerant. A condition characterized by gastrointestinal distress following the ingestion of foods which contain lactose. This is due to the relative absence of a lactose-splitting enzyme known as lactase, which is produced in part by these healthy bacteria.

Note: Another important supplement which most infants require is a high-quality strain of these beneficial microorganisms. This is especially true for those not receiving breast milk, or who have thrush, persistent diaper rash, or recurrent infections of any kind. Remember that there are no significant sources of these beneficial bacteria outside of breast milk and supplementation. Due to wide variations in the quality and potency of the many bacterial preparations being marketed today, be certain to consult with your participating Health Coach® center for more specific advice here as well.

Vitamins:
Human milk has more than ten times the amount of vitamin E, two times the vitamin A, and considerably more of the B-complex and vitamin C than does cow's milk. Potentially

as important as the above, is the fact that breast milk has not been subjected to the same intense heat that cow's milk and commercial formulas are exposed to during their pasteurization. Thus, the vitamins in mother's milk remain intact, as do the numerous enzymes whose diverse roles and functions in human health we have only just begun to study.

Minerals:
Cow's milk contains three to four times more minerals than human milk. Although this provides for the rapid growth of calves, it likely places undue stress on the human infant's metabolism. A good deal more research needs to be conducted in this area. However, those studies completed to date on the metabolism of minerals, indicate once again that quality should precede quantity here as well. The relative bio-availability of the minerals found in human breast milk appear to exceed that of cow's milk substantially. Please note that the quality and quantity of all nutrients in breast milk will vary in direct proportion to the quality of the mother's diet. This is to say that we utilize the minerals found in the milk of our own species more readily than those found in the milk of another.

"Is it possible that a food that has nurtured humankind since the earliest agrarian (agricultural) times has become harmful to us?"

Despite the obvious differences in the chemistry between human milk and that of cow's, or any other species, the single most significant argument for excluding or at least minimizing cow's milk in your or your child's diet would be the fact that it is heat processed, ie. pasteurized. Perhaps the most dramatic evidence that the application of excessive heat to certain foods, denatures various protein, enzyme and fatty acid structures was published by the Price-Pottenger Nutrition Foundation titled "Pottenger Cats". A must read for all interested in the potential impact that our overprocessing of food is having on our society.

The next most significant argument against milk's consumption is very simple: when the cow's nutrition and lifestyle is compromised, the nutritional value of their milk is similarly compromised. Cows fed on stale grains grown on chemically treated, nutrient depleted soils, raised in the absence of proper exercise and enough natural light, in confined living quarters, etc., etc... are not going to produce the highest quality milk. Therefore, commercially produced milk provides an excellent growth medium for pathogenic organisms, such as those which usually accompany unhealthy cows (which is why they are given antibiotics so frequently) and thus necessitates pasteurization/sterilization.

When commercially produced, pasteurized cows' milk is deficient in trace elements, vitamins, fatty acids, enzymes and healthy bacteria, (due to the animals lifestyle and subsequent pasteurization) it follows that those who consume it may develop faulty metabolism as well.

In summary, if raw *certified* whole milk from a truly healthy chemical-free herd is available to you and your infant, and legal where you live, and you follow the steps outlined in the following sections of this guide, observing no sign of intolerance... enjoy it and have no concerns regarding any negative health effects.

Table of Comparison

fig. 5

	Cow's Milk	Human Milk
Protein	85% casein / 15% whey.	40% casein / 60% whey.
Amino-Acid Composition	Lower in cysteine.	Higher in cysteine. Better assimilation Better detoxification
Fats & Fatty Acids	Averages about 3.5% fat. No essential fatty acids are present in significant quantities. Higher in sticky saturated fatty acids.	Contains average of 4.4% fats. Valuable essential fatty acids which help to protect against inflammations and degenerative disease.
Carbo-hydrates	Type of lactose may be harder to digest	Twice the milk sugar (energy) and easier to digest.
Vitamins Enzymes Beneficial Bacteria	10 times less vitamin E. 2 times less vitamin A. Considerably less B-complex and vitamin C.	More than 10 times the amount of vitamin E. 2 times the vitamin A. Considerably more B-complex & vitamin C.
Minerals	Has 3 to 4 times the quantity of certain minerals	The quality of minerals and their assimilation exceeds that of cow's milk
Processing	Pasteurized, homogenized and thus denatured.	None
Beneficial Bacteria	None once it has been processed.	Rich in highly beneficial immuno-protective bacteria.
Immune Enhancing Proteins	Denatured by processing.	Intact and more species specific.

Gut Ecology

The Good, the Bad and the Unnecessary

Our intestines contain many types of microorganisms, some are desirable and others are not. Nevertheless, they are all present in each of us. It is the relative proportions of the various types of these microorganisms in our intestines which determine whether there is a net beneficial effect or a net detrimental effect on each individual's health. In fact, the micro-biologists tell us that the bacteria in our intestines actually out-number the trillions of cells in our bodies!

As infants leave the womb and enter the external world, they are exposed to a host of conditions which contribute to the rapid colonization of their intestines by microorganisms. The kinds of organisms which establish themselves in the infant's gut will have a definitive effect on both the immediate and the long term health of that infant. When reviewing the factors which influence and eventually determine the make up of an infant's gut flora (microbial population) none are more significant than the foods which they receive in their first few days. This is precisely why nature has provided a very special food for all newborns in the form of colostrum. Colostrum is a unique blend of beneficial bacteria, immunoglobulins and concentrated nutrients. These constituents of colostrum working synergistically (together) serve to protect the infant's highly susceptible gastrointestinal and respiratory systems from the inroads of less desirable microorganisms or pathogens.

How many new mothers are properly briefed on the importance of their colostrum to their precious infant especially in these most crucial first few days of life? Those under the care of midwives and Health Coach® participant certainly are, as are those who attend their local LaLeche league meetings. Yet the majority of new mothers still rely solely on the advice of their medical physician and/or nursing staff, which unfortunately may have more reverence for medical technology and intervention than the natural processes at work here. In fairness, this attitude is beginning to soften in the 'church of modern medicine' and many progressive physicians and nurses are taking a position in support of these natural processes and the inherent wisdom behind them.

For those readers who still may be questioning the relative importance of infant nutrition on long term health, please consider the following information carefully.

The difference in the intestinal flora (microorganisms) in breast-fed and bottle-fed infants is substantial and has been well documented in the scientific literature.

In *breast-fed infants* the predominate intestinal bacteria are the beneficial bifida bacteria and the number of pathogenic or putrefactive bacteria is very low. The pH is also relatively low (more acidic), and there is little odour to the stools. *Bottle-fed infants*, in contrast, have much lower levels of the desirable bifida bacteria along with elevated levels of pathogenic microorganisms, including yeasts and putrefactive bacteria. Their stools also have a higher pH (more alkaline) and they have a more foul odour. These changes in the intestinal flora, established in infancy by the mode of feeding, have been demonstrated to persist in some cases even thirty years later!

What might the net effect on one's overall health be when we take into consideration the amount of toxins absorbed into the bloodstream as the result of this increased intestinal toxemia? Might this in turn place significant strain on our blood purification processes and organ systems? These include our liver, gallbladder, kidneys, spleen and lymph tissues. Is it any wonder that liver, gallbladder, kidney, spleen and various other gastro-intestinal and immune disorders abound in our culture? Could this be contributing to the host of lymph gland afflictions seen in our children these days, including inflamed tonsils, adenoids, inner ears and appendix? Such factors as antibiotic use, chlorination of our drinking water, birth control pills, alcohol and drug abuse, and ignorance of proper female hygiene*, all disrupt and interfere with the normal healthy intestinal flora of infants, children and adults similarly. Recently, it has been proposed that even ulcers may be the result of altered intestinal pH and the associated overgrowth of pathogenic bacteria. What happens to the formula-fed infants who suffer from recurrent infections and receive antibiotics as first line treatment, over and over again? Might these infants develop life-long, but often latent intestinal problems? Could this further affect their future resistance to infection and in fact predispose them to recurrent infectious conditions?

---

* It is in the vaginal canal where the infant's sterile systems first contact any microorganisms. If there is not a healthy balance of the right bacteria here, and instead there is an overgrowth of yeast or pathogenic organisms, this can have an adverse affect on your infant. There are several important steps which you can take to ensure that this first exposure to "bugs" is more favourable than hostile. For more information on the importance of female hygiene, please contact your participating Health Coach® center and ask for the information on (P.E.P. Step) "Dietary Considerations for Normalization of Intestinal and Vaginal Flora".

What if there were other approaches to these health challenges which did not disrupt bodily functions? What if these complimentary approaches favoured and enhanced the infant's natural defense mechanisms?

In all but the purely emergency cases, more comprehensive approaches focused on removing the cause and not simply treating the effects, are both available and warranted in dealing with our children's health. For further understanding here, I refer you once again to the P.E.P. articles: "Health vs Disease" and "Understanding the Action of Drugs in Relation to Natural Laws".

Weaning Without Worries!

How long do you breast-feed and when do you introduce solid foods?

The following recommendations presume you, the mother, are eating the best possible diet, rich in the essential fatty acids, a wide variety of whole unprocessed foods and taking the ratio-balanced, broad spectrum, high quality, multiple vitamin and mineral supplement which has been prescribed by your participating Health Coach® center. I urge all prospective and current parents to study and do their best to implement the nutritional principles explained in our text <u>Functional Dietetics</u>. This manual outlines the strategy for determining the diet which is best for you as an adult. Doing so greatly reduces the likelihood of your infant failing to thrive or reacting to your breast milk unfavourably. Too many mothers have discontinued breast-feeding due to infant irritability, when all they had to do was understand and follow the dietary practices outlined in <u>Functional Dietetics</u>. If you run into any difficulties with breast-feeding or with your infant's tolerance of your milk, be certain to notify your nutrition-oriented health professional (Health Coach® participant) immediately for their input and support. I also encourage new mothers to contact their local La Leche League. Their book <u>The Womanly Art of Breast-Feeding</u> offers helpful information around the challenges some may face with breast-feeding.

Up to 6 Months of Age

Breast-feeding alone can and will provide optimal nutrition for your infant providing the previously stated guidelines are being followed by Mom! Introducing other beverages or solid foods during this period is seldom necessary. Do not supplement your infant's diet with vitamins or minerals or even water at this time unless your health professional has prescribed something specifically. A number of factors are involved here which necessitate your coach's input. The exception here is if your infant has diarrhea and/or vomitting and is in risk of dehydration. In these cases be certain to provide your infant water or diluted fruit juice and contact your doctor immediately.

From 6 to 9 Months of Age

Six months is generally the earliest age for foods and beverages other than breast milk to be introduced into your infant's diet. However, many infants are still fine on breast milk alone throughout this period. If your child is no longer satisfied with just breast milk and demands to be fed with increasing frequency, or is failing to thrive, you may find it necessary to introduce other foods at this time (see the following pages). If your baby is happy, growing normally (approximately 1 to 1.5 pounds per month), and appears to be satisfied, there is no advantage to the introduction of any other foods at this point. Conversely, as discussed in the section on Infant Digestion, introducing new foods prematurely could result in considerable detriment.

If they have not done so already, your participating Health Coach® or nutrition-oriented health professional will likely suggest that you begin to supplement your infant's diet with a multiple vitamin preparation during this period. Micellized vitamins are considered the best, as they have absorption characteristics similar to those vitamins occurring naturally in breast milk. The exception here will be when your infant shows any signs of mineral insufficiency on evaluation. In these cases, as minerals can not be micellized, other preparations will be prescribed.

This is an area of vital importance to your infant's health. **Nutrient insufficiencies may not become apparent until long after any damage has been done.** Please don't play roulette with your infant's health. Get accurate direction here. Be certain to consult with a qualified health professional regarding the specific dosages and to ensure proper quality control.

Note: From this point on I will use the term 'health coach' to refer to the health professional you have chosen as your coach and advisor. It will be understood that if they have not participated in our Infant Nutrition training their advice may well differ from the teachings of Health Coach® Systems.

From 9 to 12 Months of Age

Most infants begin to insist on additional foods during this period. The infant's digestive system has usually developed sufficiently to handle some other-than-breast-milk foods. Teeth are forming, assisting mastication and salivary secretions have increased substantially. If breast milk production is still plentiful and it will be if you are following the nutritional guidelines found in <u>Functional Dietetics</u>, by all means continue nursing your infant. Breast milk is still the front runner in nutritious foods by a substantial margin and as such, other foods are given in addition to breast milk, not vice versa.

Introducing New Foods Properly

In order to fully appreciate the food introduction process and its importance, please consider the following points thoughtfully.

Just as no two infants are identical physically (even 'identical' twins) no two infants have identical nutritional needs. Determining just what to feed your infant is a process requiring, careful study, close observation and accurate recording and good professional coaching. We have discussed at some length the impact which improper nutrition can have on your infant, now here is how to minimize the risk of this actually happening.

Remember, as you introduce foods which your infant does not seem to tolerate, there are many reasons for such intolerance. If your infant has responded poorly to a food, but not severely, and this food is a whole natural food which you would like to include in their diet, simply leave that food out of the diet for several weeks and then introduce it again. If it is still not tolerated, leave it out for at least three months before trying it again; but if there are no such signs at this time, it may then be included in your infant's *rotational** diet plan. As you find specific foods which do not agree with your infant, please refer to the food family groupings in Appendix C. This will allow you to identify that food's specific food family, so that you can watch for similar intolerance of the other foods found in that family. This intra-family intolerance is quite common.

---

* Variety is the spice of life and the backbone of a complete nutrition plan. Rotating foods, eating them 2-3 times weekly vs 2-3 times daily helps to ensure that your infant receives a wider variety of foods. This is much easier as you identify a number of foods which they tolerate.

Also note that as **you introduce foods with lower water content than that of breast milk you should begin to supplement with pure water, but not before.** Numerous studies have demonstrated that such supplementation with water is not necessary, nor desirable when the infant is on breast milk alone. The exception to this would be the infant who is displaying signs of dehydration: infrequent and concentrated urine, hard stools, dry skin and/or puffy swollen tongue. Fortunately this is rare in the absence of diarrhea and/ or vomiting. If you suspect any such problem, begin to supplement feedings with pure water and contact your health coach immediately. To determine accurately what foods are best for your infant, follow the steps below closely.

Start with only one food at a time and continue that one food for at least four days provided there are no signs of intolerance. Observe closely for any of the following common signs of intolerance or allergy.

- Redness around the mouth, usually within one or two hours of ingestion, or twelve to twenty-four hours later around the anus.
- Abdominal bloating, gas and distension (yes indeed this is common, but it is certainly not a healthy sign).
- Irritability, fussiness, overactivity, awakes more frequently through the night, often crying or screaming (due to intestinal discomfort).
- Constipation, diarrhea or foul odour to the stools. Discomfort prior to passing stools. (No this is not normal or healthy, even if it is common.)
- Frequent regurgitation of foods, ie. spitting up.
- Nasal and/or chest congestion and catarrh (runny nose).
- Red, chapped and/or inflamed eczema-like skin, on face, groin, bottom, or virtually anywhere on the body.

If you observe any of these signs, discontinue the food, wait until the signs and symptoms have cleared and then go on to the next food. Depending on the severity of the reaction, you may or may not wish to try it again in the future, in order to confirm its effect. **Any signs or symptoms which do not clear rapidly on withdrawal of that food, are to be discussed with your health coach promptly.**

Foods to Start First

Fruits

Start wherever possible with freshly prepared juices rather than the whole mashed foods, and dilute them by using 1 part juice to 2 parts pure water. Just give 1 to 2 teaspoons of the diluted juice initially and observe the response before offering more the next time. I suggest beginning with *fresh* fruit juices first, as they are easiest to digest and are readily accepted by most infants. They are relatively sweet and of a texture similar to that of breast milk. In the absence of any of the previously discussed signs of intolerance, you may then proceed to introduce the freshly mashed or pureed ripe fruits.

There are infants who do not tolerate certain fruits well, so on any signs of intolerance (colic, diarrhea, facial or diaper rash, etc) just leave those fruits and proceed with the others or even vegetables in their place.

Fruits in season and regionally-grown are preferred and are usually better tolerated by your infant. Choose organically grown fruits whenever possible and be certain to scrub the fruit skins well with hot water and an organic cleanser which has been specifically formulated to remove any pesticide and/or herbicide residues which may be present. Refer to the P.E.P. Step "Washing Your Fruits, Vegetables, Grains, Legumes" for details here.)

Some propose removal of the skins on all fruits as the solution to the chemical residues which may be present. Unfortunately the majority of micronutrients which are present in fruits lie within the skin, the outermost portion of the fruit and within their seeds. The peeling and coring of fruit leaves only the high carbohydrate pulp to provide for your infant's much broader nutritional needs. Therefore, my recommendations here are as follows:

- Begin with the freshly extracted juice of one of the juicier fruits (pears, peaches, nectarines, melons, etc.). Dilute it 2 parts pure water to 1 part fresh juice. Give this several times on Day 1 and observe for any signs or symptoms of intolerance. In their absence, proceed to:

  Peel and core that particular fruit and/or remove the rind or seeds from its 'flesh'. Puree the 'flesh' only, at first, to as fine a texture as possible. Add water to thin if necessary as many infants are very particular about food textures and it may take some time to identify your infant's preferences here. Please do not be too quick to interpret your infant's initial rejection of any food as a dislike of its taste. In many cases it is simply the texture of the food which they are reacting to. Be creative here and do some experimenting with a variety of textures. Feed your infant several teaspoons of this fresh fruit puree, closely observing for any adverse response once again. If all is clear, that particular fruit may be included in your infant's diet for several consecutive days. If all remains clear, it may now become part of your infant's diet. Then proceed to the next fruit.

  Because the whole fresh fruit is most desirable in all

but those obvious examples where the skins (as with citrus), the rinds (as with melons) or the pits (as with peaches, plums, cherries, etc.) are not palatable, you may proceed to puree the whole fruit and then put it through a fine mesh strainer whenever possible. Some may be curious as to why one might choose to include the seeds of citrus or melons for example when they are so bitter. First and most importantly, it is from the seeds of all plants that new life springs forth and as such, they are exceptional in nutrient value. Secondly the bitter tasting substances in many foods serve as digestive tonics, stimulating the flow of a variety of intestinal secretions which aid your infant's digestion (and yours for that matter). Thirdly, recent studies have demonstrated important anti-bacterial, anti-viral and anti-parasitic properties in the seeds of such common fruits and vegetables as grapefruits and pumpkins. There are therefore, a number of good reasons to include these little bundles of nutrition in our diets.

The reader is also cautioned here, that while a little is good, it does not always follow that more is better. Use common sense and follow Mother Nature's lead. Please do not go collecting your friends' and neighbours' discarded seeds and feed them to your family! Just eat more whole foods, where appropriate. Another consideration here is that **parts of many seeds are quite woody and if not pulverized completely to pulp could be irritating to an infant's, or even an adult's, digestive system.** In the worst case scenario, **they could even become lodged in the throat of an infant and choke them.** With this in mind, I recommend that if you are going to provide your infants with the benefits of seeds in their diet, that you take proper care in their preparation.

The only way to effectively pulverize these woody seeds, to this author's knowledge, is with a Vita-Mix food processor. Proper use of the Vita-Mix* will make much of your food preparation for your infant a breeze. Your whole family would benefit from the way this unit facilitates the preparation of whole fruits, vegetables, seeds and grains. Unfortunately the recipe book, which comes with the unit, is replete with highly processed ingredients and thus receives no endorsement from this author. It does provide you however, with enough guidelines to allow you to apply a broader understanding of whole food nutrition to its many uses. Our family and friends enjoy and appreciate the delightful by-products of our Vita-Mix unit. **Even when using a Vita-Mix, you must put your infant's foods through a fine mesh strainer to ensure its safety.**

After introducing a variety of fruits in the above fashion, begin to rotate the various types and families of fruits (see Appendix C, The Diversified Rotation Diet). This helps ensure better nutrition and serves to minimize the intolerances which so often arise when dietary patterns are too monotonous.

A rotational diet plan is best accomplished by laying out 4-day menus, each being unique in composition and from different food families, for example:

Day 1   Breast milk plus peaches and apricots
Day 2   Breast milk plus strawberries and raspberries
Day 3   Breast milk plus apples and pears
Day 4   Breast milk plus papaya and mangos

This advance menu planning will also facilitate more effective grocery shopping.

---

* *To order a Vita-Mix unit or receive information call:*
   The Vita-Mix Corporation - 8615 Usher Road
   216-235-4840   Olmsted Falls, Ohio 44138

To recap, the reasons for starting with fruits are as follows:

- they require very little digestion for adequate absorption and utilization
- they contain an abundance of vitamins and minerals
- they are an excellent source of energy as they are rich in natural carbohydrates (fruit sugars)
- they are high in water content, and most infants take to them readily
- they have a similar protein content to breast milk

It must also be noted here that all fruits are not created equal. There are four distinct sub-categories of fruits: neutral, sweet, acid and sub-acid. It is suggested that you begin with the neutral or sub-acid categories first, as the acid category may be too acid for some infants and the sweet category are not easily juiced. Each of these categories is digested better when eaten separately, with the sweet and acid groups not mixing well together at all. There are also two families of fruits which are best eaten alone, separate from all other foods. They are the citrus and the melon families. Melons, simply because they do not digest well with the others, and citrus, likely because they are not allowed to ripen on the tree, they are almost always dyed and sprayed with mold retardants etc. Tree-ripened, organically grown citrus would likely be tolerated better.

Please use fresh ripe fruits (not canned) and organically grown where possible. If fresh are not available, unsweetened frozen fruit are your next best choice.

Babies will generally accept new food best midway between breast feedings, so this is a good time to present them. They are also digested better apart from other foods, including breast milk. (ie. At least 1 to 1-1/2 hours after a feeding.) I do not advocate or endorse the *frequent* use of fruit juice bottle-feedings for infants. The exception being those beverages made by blending fresh fruit puree with pure water. Far too many infants develop rotten teeth and insatiable 'sweet tooths' as the result of the excessive consumption of the relatively acidic fruit sugar from juices. Just pause to consider how many apples or oranges went into that eight ounces of juice, and how long would it have taken the infant to eat that many fruits whole! The excessive consumption of over processed liquid calories is perhaps the primary reason for the high incidence of undernourished children today. These children usually have fussy palates and are reluctant to eat whole natural, low sugar foods such as: seeds, nuts, vegetables, lentils, legumes and whole grains. Commercially prepared fruit juices are little more than empty liquid calories, which discourage more healthful eating patterns.

Once again, the best choices here are whole fruit purees, or beverages made by adding pure water to these. Please avoid the commercially processed juices. If your child is thirsty, give them pure water, not processed fruit juice. If hungry, your child deserves *whole* foods. Several other healthy whole food beverages will be discussed shortly.

Vegetables

Now that you have introduced fruits (as tolerated) to your infant, you may begin to add vegetables. This is your best opportunity to develop your infant's palate properly. (ie. In the absence of any commercially processed foods, often laden with concentrated sugars and artificial flavourings.)

Start by introducing the *freshly prepared* juices of carrots, or any of the following vegetables: squash, carrots, beets, celery, cucumber, all leafy greens, parsley, and zucchini. Carrot is a good starting point as it is uniquely sweet and

Classification of Natural Fruits

ACID	SWEET	SUB-ACID
Acerola	Banana	Akee
Carambola	Canistel	Apple
Ceylon Gooseberry	Carob	Pear
Cranberry	Date	Blackberry
Currant	Durian	Cactus Fruit
Gooseberry	Fig	Carissa
Grapefruit*	Jakfruit	Ceriman
Kumquat	Litchi (dried)	Cherimoya
Lemon*	Mammea	Cherry
Lime*	Prune	Elderberry
Loganberry	Raisin	Feijoa
Loquat	Sapodilla	Grape
Medlar	Sapote	Guava
Orange*	Apricot	Huckleberry
Pineapple		Jaboticaba
Pitanga		Jujube
Pomegranate	**NEUTRAL**	Juneberry
Shaddock		Litchi (fresh)
Sour Apples	Melons (all)*	Mango
Strawberry		Mulberry
Tamarind		Marang
Tangerine		Nectarine
Tomato*		Plum
Umkokola		Paw Paw
Kiwi		Peach
		Persimmon
		Ramontchi
		Raspberry
		Soursop
		Star Apple
*Citrus and melons are best digested		Sugar Apple
when eaten separately (by themselves).		Papaya

palatable. Other vegetables may be juiced and added to your carrot juice base as you continue your vegetable introductions.

Juices are extremely concentrated sources of nutrients and food energy. As such, they are best diluted by 4 parts pure water to 1 part fresh juice initially. When you are certain of their tolerance (2 to 4 days later), the concentration may be slowly increased to 1 part pure water to 1 part juice, and in some cases no dilution at all. This will depend on your infant's growth and appetite for other foods and is up to you and your health coach to determine.

Summary:

Use freshly prepared carrot juice as your base. I suggest preparing 2 ounces and diluting it with 8 ounces of pure water. This can be offered by teaspoon, dropper or by bottle but only 1 or 2 ounces to start, until you are sure of your infant's tolerance. Then begin to juice other vegetables, one at a time, similar to the routine with fruits, only this time you are adding the new juice to your carrot juice base to enhance its taste and acceptance by your infant. In the rare case where your infant does not tolerate the carrot juice, you may try fresh apple juice as the base for your *vegetable cocktails*. Be aware that apples also can be allergenic, despite their excellent nutritional value. If neither work out, just skip the juice phase and continue with the fresh vegetable purees as follows.

For those who are newcomers to juicing, after carrot, celery, cucumber, zucchini and beet are next on the veggie juice palatability scale. With these and all other vegetable juices, a little goes a long way. Just observe how much of the whole vegetable is required to produce even one ounce of juice. That is often all that is needed. Just as an aside, celery's relative alkalinity, makes it a good natural buffer to any of the more acid juices, like tomato.

As with fruits, whole is better than part, so progress to whole vegetable purees as soon as your infant will accept them, just watch closely to ensure tolerance. Please don't cook any vegetables that you don't have to! Vegetables do not have to be sterilized before they are eaten. It is much more important that the vital nutrients and enzymes in them remain intact. Bake or steam only those starchier vegetables which might be difficult to digest raw or to puree properly. These include: potatoes, turnip, squash, parsnips and beets, but be sure not to overcook them. The mustard family is usually better tolerated when steamed lightly (cabbage, cauliflower, broccoli, etc. See #24 on page 96). If bloating or colic results, let the symptoms clear, then try them again more thoroughly steamed.

Once you have discovered a variety of well-tolerated vegetables, begin to rotate these on your 4-day menu plan as with fruits (see Appendix C, page 93).

Note: It is best not to give fruits and vegetables together at one meal, as this may disrupt proper digestion. Fruits are best eaten before other foods, earlier in the day. This is true for adults as well.

Seeds and Nuts

Whether you have continued to breast-feed or not will determine when you will begin introducing the following highly nutritious, protein and mineral rich seed and nut preparations. In the interest of your infant's health I suggest that breast-feeding be continued, and that you introduce this next category of foods after both fruits and vegetables, and generally between nine and twelve months of age. If breast-feeding is decreased or discontinued earlier than this, then introduce them at that time. The frequency of the use of seeds and nuts will depend on a number of factors. These include:

- your infant's age
- your infant's tolerance of other foods and the relatively availability of those foods
- your infant's palate
- your infant's growth
- your breast-feeding schedule
- the specific feedback of your health coach

The following seed and nut preparations provide a balance of proteins, essential fatty acids, complex carbohydrates and valuable minerals very similar to that of breast milk.

The most nutritious seeds are fresh, raw: flax, sesame, sunflower, and pumpkin. The flax seeds are higher in the mucilaginous fibers which affect the consistency of beverages, so grind these to powder and add them to pureed fruit or vegetables, at least until grain purees are introduced at a later date. All seeds can then be ground and added to these foods readily. All seeds must be liquified and strained or ground into a fine paste for your infant to receive their full value and to prevent any possibility of choking. The tiny seeds of flax and sesame are best ground in a seed/coffee bean grinder or a Vita-Mix first, and then added to foods or to blender drinks. A blender alone is not adequate for their complete breakdown and they can not be digested properly unless finely ground. Inexpensive electric grinders are made by companies such as Braun and Moulinex, primarily for coffee beans, but they do an excellent job on these tiny seeds. Now... onto the nuts.

The more nutritious nuts are fresh, raw almonds, walnuts and filberts (hazelnuts). All of these blend easily in a standard blender.

All seeds and nuts are rich in nutritious oils, however these oils become rancid rapidly upon exposure to light, heat and air. Thus, when purchasing nuts and seeds, look for uniform colour, and always taste them for freshness. Flax and sesame seeds are very stable until ground and then they are to be used immediately or at least kept in your freezer. Pumpkin seeds are less stable and must be kept cold and away from light.

Almonds are the most stable of the nuts and keep quite well even after they have been shelled. The same is not true for other nuts and thus they are best when purchased in the shells and removed at the time of consumption. This is not very practical for most however, so the next best option is to purchase them shelled, but still whole, from stores where they move fast and are kept refrigerated. Rancid oils are relatively toxic and have no place in your infant's diet. Always refrigerate seeds, nuts, their butters and milks... that's right, you can make delicious milks from seeds and/or nuts.

Be creative and make your own combination of seed and nut milks varying the consistency according to your infant's demands and palate. Originally, make the consistency very thin by adding more water and strain the blended liquid through a cheese cloth or fine mesh strainer in order to mimic the consistency of breast milk. You may gradually increase the preparation's consistency by adding less water, eventually using it as a puree, paste or spread. Tahini (ground sesame seeds) and almond butter (ground almonds) are delicious and nutritious, especially when prepared at home, thus ensuring the freshness of their oils. These are preferred to peanut butter, which is both a common allergen and a possible toxin due to the frequent presence of mold residues. The almond and sesame alternatives are also more nutritious.

For starters, blend 3 tablespoons of blanched (skinless) almonds with 2 cups of lukewarm pure water (avoid feeding yourself or your infant tap water unless you are certain of its purity -- see Functional Dietetics, section on Water Quality, pages 20-21). Once blended well, some sweetener may be required to entice your infant. If this is the case, proceed as follows. Place 2 heaping tablespoons of raisins (organically grown and paraffin-free if available) in 1 cup of pure water and simmer for 5 minutes. This will serve to denature any potential mold residues which can occur on the raisins (or any dried fruits) and will partially re-hydrate the raisins, making them easier to blend.

If raisins are not tolerated well by your infant, then substitute 1 tablespoon of unsulfered molasses here. Both raisins and molasses are good sources of iron, which along with the iron-rich seeds, make these seed milks an excellent source of this valuable nutrient. Beets are also a good source of iron (a nutrient which is not abundant in many of the foods appropriate for early infant feedings). An ounce of freshly grated beets here increases the nutritional value of these homemade formulas. Add the raisins and their now sweetened water (if no wax, etc. is present) to the nut milk along with the grated beets and thoroughly liquify. If your infant is still hesitant, add a little unsulfured blackstrap molasses or pasteurized honey. Almond milk is a fine supplement for the mother who is weaning her infant, or for the infant who has been on commercial infant formulas day after day. Please recall our discussion of how such constant repetition can contribute to the development of allergies and intolerance to these frequently eaten foods.

With this in mind, the reader is encouraged to alternate using sesame, sunflower or pumpkin seeds for the almonds when making these seed or nut milks. For a super nutritious and delicious hypo-allergenic formula, suitable for infant and adults alike, refer to Appendix D page 99 "The Coach's Super Formula". Remembering that seeds and nuts are very concentrated sources of both energy and nutrients, therefore only small amounts need to be consumed at any one time. Try this beverage for yourself and your family as an alternate to dairy. **Remember, I still encourage you to test your infant's tolerance of each of the ingredients separately first, just as I have been coaching you to do.**

Your Baby's First Birthday!

My genuine respect and congratulations are extended to those parents who have continued to breast-feed throughout this first year and who have successfully introduced a number of fresh fruits, vegetables and, more recently, some seed and nut milks. If you have followed the preceding advice closely and you have consulted regularly with your health coach regarding your infant's progress, you will in all likelihood have a child who sleeps well through the night, has a pleasant disposition, demonstrates good growth and development, learns readily and seldom gets very ill. If you do not wish to wean your child yet, simply continue to breast-feed for as long as you wish (eighteen to twenty-four months is not unusual in many cultures around the world). For those who have for one reason or another been unable to follow the 'ideal' guidelines thus far, take heart, as excellent health can still await your infant. Just be sure to consult with your health coach regarding your best alternatives given your specific circumstances and challenges. If they have participated in the Health Coach® System Infant Nutrition training, they have been well trained to share any compensatory strategies with you which may be required to maximize your infant's health. Above all, take comfort in that you have done the best you can given your unique situations and that by following even some of these guidelines, you have very likely given your infant a much better start than most of us received. Keep doing your very best and feel good about the love and care which you are demonstrating for your little "bundle of miracles".

For those of you who decide to wean your child at this point, slowly cut back the number of breast-feedings and increase the frequency and the amount of other foods. Please offer only healthy, fresh, whole food preparations. If there is sufficient variety, your child will get plenty to eat. All too many well-intentioned (but mis-informed) parents offer their infants refined, processed, sweetened and otherwise adulterated foods in their efforts to encourage them to eat more and to grow faster. This only encourages horizontal growth; that of adipose tissue (fat), and in reality, it may stunt the infant's true growth and development. This can occur as a direct result of displacing the nutrient-rich, whole, natural foods with the calorie-rich, nutrient-poor substitutes. Once again, I urge you to consider quality here, before quantity.

When to Introduce Grains

Considerable variation exists from infant to infant here, but studies indicate that grains are less likely to be digested properly until between 1 and 1-1/2 years of age. My advice to you is to hold off the introduction of grains as long as your child is content and developing normally. Remember that vegetables are the most important foods we eat. Very few of us have eaten even half the amount of vegetables which we ideally should have. Many rush the introduction of grains due to convenience. As parents, you must decide for yourselves where your priorities lie, with the health of your infant or with convenience? With the right coaching and a little experience, eating properly seldom takes more time, but it does require some thought and preparation in advance of meal times.

Because of the frequency of allergy and intolerance to wheat and the other gluten-containing grains (barley, oats, rye and triticale), it is suggested that you introduce these last. Corn, although it does not contain any gluten, is another common allergen and as such, is suggested for later introduction as well.

This leaves the non-gluten grains of: rice (all types),

millet, quinoa and amaranth for introduction first, followed by buckwheat, a very low-gluten grain. All of these can be initially introduced as grain milks. Just cook them as per the "Grain Preparation Chart", Appendix a page 89), then blend with pure water, add a little of one of the sweeteners suggested for the seed and nut milks, put it through a fine strainer or cheesecloth and presto, another non-allergenic, highly nutritious beverage for your infant. As with the seed/nut milks, you will likely have to widen the opening in the bottle nipple to allow for the increased consistency. Be careful here not to open it too much though or your infant will receive it too fast and potentially miss the salivary phase of digestion. You may also simply choose to cook these grains as porridges, pureeing and serving them as pablum. Sweeten as previously discussed but only if your infant insists. Remember that organic (paraffin and sulphur-free) raisins are the sweetener of choice, due to their iron content.

An alternative method of increasing the palatability of grains is to mix them with some pureed ripe fruits for their natural sweetness. A word of caution here though, as the combining of significant amounts of fruit can impair the digestion of the starchy grains and lead to their fermentation in your infant's intestines. The signs of this include: bloating, gas, irritability (usually) and foul stools. In more severe cases, vomiting or diarrhea may occur. I suggest that all parents get into the habit of gently palpating their infant's abdomen and observing it for bloating, and increased pressure. Healthy infants' abdomens are flat when they are resting on their backs. Your health coach will assist you in making these small yet important distinctions more accurately.

Consult the food combining chart in Appendix A page 86 for the list of high water content vegetables, suitable for eating with meals containing grains or starchy vegetables. This chart of food combinations represents the 'best choice' scenarios and you are encouraged to study it and to adhere to its guidelines where and whenever circumstances permit. However, as your Health Coach will explain to you further, if you find that you must bend these rules to get nutritious foods into your infant, then do so. Just be sure to do your best here and see that you only bend these rules out of necessity, not convenience, as they do make a difference in your infant's comfort and health.

As your infant's teeth appear and their ability to chew properly develops, there are many creative ways to prepare these grain-vegetable meals. For dozens of such recipes, consult the food preparation manual titled Guilt-free Indulgence, An Art Worth Mastering. This book and its guidelines form an integral part of the Health Coach® System.

"But Doctor, I can't continue breast-feeding... so now what?"

If your infant is at least four months of age, simply begin the seed and nut milks first, and then "The Coach's Super Formula" (Appendix D page 99). Then proceed with the fruits and vegetables as outlined earlier in this text. Rest assured that your health coach will assist you here in monitoring your infant's development and growth (or find a new one...now!).

If your infant is less than four months of age or does not receive the seed and nut milks well, provide your child with the closest animal milk to that of human's, ie. goat's milk. As mentioned in our discussion around the relative suitability of other species' milk for human infants, fresh raw certified goat's milk is certainly preferable to that which has been pasteurized and homogenized. Introduce the 'best available' goat's milk by diluting it with 3 parts pure water to 1 part whole goat's milk. If well tolerated, as evidenced by no significant change in stool odour, form or frequency, and the absence of bloating, colic, rash, regurgitation or irritability, etc., continue as directed above, replacing regular breast-feedings with the diluted goat's milk. How much? Let your infant decide how much milk. Just be sure to present fruits and vegetables at four to six months so all of your child's calories are not liquid alone. You can gradually over the course of 7 to 14 days, increase the concentration of the goat's milk to 2 parts goat's milk to 1 part pure water. Remember to separate as much as possible the milk feedings from the vegetable or fruit feedings. If you keep these 3 food groups as separate meals, your infant will digest them much better.

There is some concern as to the iron and folic acid content of goat's milk. Adding a liquid multiple vitamin and mineral supplement here can ensure adequate levels of these and other key nutrients.

What if goat's milk is not tolerated? If goat's milk is not tolerated and the seed and nut milks are not received well, then proceed to introduce:

1) a pre-digested lactose-free commercially prepared infant formula such as Nutramigen or Alimentum

2) a milk and lactose-free soy based formula such as Prosobee or Isomil

But what about plain soymilk you ask? Make no mistake, plain soymilk is not an adequate substitute by itself. If the infant is under four months of age and has not tolerated (or has refused) goat's milk, then it is suggested that you try them on one of the infant formulas mentioned above. These cases warrant more comprehensive evaluation by your health coach, so be certain to consult directly with them.

If you are still having challenges here, or if you are just curious as to whether your infant could tolerate the occasional ingestion of dairy products, you may try cow's milk, but begin by mixing low-lactose 'live-culture' yogurt with enough warm water to create a milk-like consistency and observe their tolerance to this first (see Appendix A page 87). This type of yogurt is the easiest dairy product to digest and if it is not tolerated well, then other forms of dairy will not be either. If the yogurt is tolerated well, you may add some milk to your infant's program. Initially add 3 parts pure water to 1 part whole milk and gradually increase to 2 parts milk to 1 part pure water. You may markedly improve the nutritional value of these cow's milk feedings by adding 1/2 teaspoon of fresh, properly processed flax seed oil (refer to Functional Dietetics, section on Fats and Oils) to each 8 oz. bottle of milk. In addition, I suggest that you add 1/2 teaspoon of a high-quality beneficial bacteria preparation, containing 2 parts bifidus to 1 part lactobacillus acidophillus. The addition of flax oil and beneficial bacteria is also recommended with the use of the above mentioned infant formulas.

Remember to always consult your health coach before supplementing *anything* to your infant's diet. Once again I caution the reader against overuse of any singular food here, so unless none of the other aforementioned preparations were tolerated, please rotate all dairy products on the usual 4-day plan. ie. Only offer them once or twice a week to your infant.

Introducing Lentils, Legumes and the Gluten Grains

Whenever you decide to introduce these more concentrated complex carbohydrates, please take into consideration the information provided earlier on infant digestion. Recall that their ability to adequately digest starchy foods before the age of 1 to 1-1/2 years or the appearance of their first molars is quite limited.

These whole foods are readily available in most health food stores in their organic form (relatively free from pesticides, insecticides and herbicides). They are inexpensive and second only to the fresh fruits, vegetables, seeds, nuts and non-gluten grains discussed earlier with respect to their nutritional value... *when digested properly.*

The most nutritious method of preparing the grains is by first sprouting them. Then puree them in a blender or Vita-Mix to compensate for ongoing limitations in your infant's ability to chew them properly. When these gluten grains are sprouted they become both more nutritious and easier to digest. Adding fresh carrots or carrot juice to the pureed sprouts improves both their taste and their nutritional value. Sprouting trays and instructions on their use are available at your local health food store. A word of caution here as bean sprouts can be toxic if consumed too frequently, so stick to the grain sprouts instead.

When cooking your grains, lentils or legumes, rinse them thoroughly and then, whenever possible, soak them in pure water before simmering them. The length of time you soak them depends on the nature of the food, as you are soaking to both reduce cooking time and to improve their digestibility. The harder the grain, pea or bean, the longer you soak them; the longer you soak, the less you cook; the less you cook, the less nutrients you destroy and the less energy that you use. (Refer to the Grain and Legume Preparation Charts, Appendix A page 89 to 91.)

Explore the whole gluten grains: oat groats, pot barley, rye kernels, buckwheat, spelt, triticale and whole wheat berries first here as they are more nutritious. Soak and simmer them as mentioned earlier, then put them in the blender (to compensate for your infant's lack of 'grinding' teeth) and add a little seed and/or nut milk to improve their consistency and flavour. Your other choice in preparing grains is to grind your grains before simmering them, thus eliminating the need for soaking or excessive cooking. Please consider the purchase of a Vita-Mix or a grain mill, as the highly nutritious essential fatty acids found in grains and seeds are rapidly destroyed on exposure to light, heat and oxygen. Therefore, any milling should ideally take place in one's kitchen, just before preparation, to ensure maximum nutritional benefit and the best possible flavour. Because of its versatility, the Vita-Mix is my first choice here, but enough grains to meet your infant's needs can be ground in seconds with a $20 electric 'coffee grinder'.

I do not advocate nurturing your infant's sweet tooth, but if you must, then you may sweeten these preparations by using a tiny amount of honey, unsulphured blackstrap molasses, maple syrup, pureed raisins or ripe fruit, as explained earlier. Just recall that each of these may interfere to some extent with proper digestion and may place unnecessary stress on your infant's blood sugar regulating mechanisms. Some infants handle this added stress with little trouble, while others suffer considerably physically and/or emotionally.

As your child gets older and is able to chew properly, begin to add grains, lentils and legumes to salads and steamed vegetable dishes. Many cultures around the world enjoy grain, lentil and vegetable combinations as staples in their diets. Once again I refer you to the cookbook Guilt-free Indulgence, An Art Worth Mastering for assistance in the creative preparation of a more plant-based diet. Its largely cholesterol-free, dairy-free, wheat-free, yeast-free and delicious recipes will delight your palate, while satisfying the principles of healthful eating.

Often adding nutritious dressings or sauces to salads and/or grains helps to encourage your children (and yourself) to eat more of these important foods. Refer to the sample recipes in Appendix D, modified for infants from the aforementioned cookbook or simply use other wholesome ingredients to create your own dressings and sauces. The oils must be fresh and rich in the essential fatty acids, having been protected from the rancidifying effects of light, air and heat during their processing. How can you identify these oils? They are in dark bottles (shielded from light) with both the pressing date and the expiry date indicated clearly on them. There should not be more than six months between these dates if the oil is truly 'unprocessed'. Another indication is the full fresh flavor of the properly extracted oils. Flax oil has the highest nutrient value of all the oils, being richest in the relatively rare omega-3 series precursor, alpha-linolenic acid. But please don't cook or fry with these delicate vegetable oils, as this not only denatures them, but it often makes them toxic (refer to Functional Dietetics, section on Fats and Oils). If you must heat or cook with an oil use the more heat stable yet nutritious (when processed properly) sesame, safflower or olive oils. Sesame will hold up the best under the higher heat of woks and stir-fries. When used for these purposes, adding water to the oil reduces the temperature required to cook , and the addition of garlic pieces slows the oxidation (spoiling) of the oils when exposed to heat and air.

Flesh Foods: Separating Fact from Fantasy

We **generally** do not **need** to include flesh foods in our diets to maintain our health. In fact, more and more studies are demonstrating exceptionally low disease and mortality rates in those who choose not to eat animal flesh. On the other hand, to my knowledge, there have not been any studies demonstrating significant detrimental effects from the truly moderate consumption of properly prepared wild or organically-raised, low-fat minimally processed flesh foods from healthy animals. Indeed, Dr. Weston Price, after studying various populations around the world, found exceptional health in many who consumed meat-based diets. The key distinction here is that these meat-based diets were essentially non-processed, even with respect to heating or cooking. The animal products consumed were fresh, minimally cooked and from animals raised naturally. The most nutritious flesh foods include: cold water ocean fish, wild game, buffalo, lamb, drug-free free-range poultry (without the skin), and lean organically raised beef. There is no arguing the fact that flesh foods are very concentrated sources of many valuable nutrients including: proteins, vitamins and minerals, (all of which may be obtained from other non-flesh foods I must add).

The question of the appropriateness of flesh foods or dairy products for human consumption is not as cut and dried as either the vegetarian groups or the meat producers would lead us to believe. Moral issues aside for the moment, some individuals, due to their genetics, digest these animal-based foods well and experience better health when including them in their regular diet, while others, also due to genetic variation, experience superior health when avoiding either flesh foods or dairy products or both. This is not a question of good or bad or right or wrong, it is a question of individual needs and preferences. It is my personal opinion that humans, as a species, will eventually evolve to more vegetarian lifestyles but this will take many generations of continued genetic adaptation. It is not something that we can, or should, force on anyone else. Let us instead focus on genuine respect for each individual's uniqueness and let us endeavour to pay more attention to our own body's subtle cues in an attempt to discern which food and lifestyle choices are most appropriate for ourselves and our infants.

If you are inclined to introduce some of the flesh foods to your infant, (eggs fall into this category as well) you may do so after nine months of age, but it is preferable to wait until after his/her first birthday, watching closely for any signs of intolerance. The most common problem is the inability to digest them. This would usually be evidenced by bloating, gas, a foul odour to your infant's stools and often smaller, harder stools.

My greatest concern around the consumption of animal products is the insidious bio-accumulation of insecticide, pesticide, herbicide, drug and heavy metal contaminants which have become so prevalent in our food chain. This is especially true of the flesh of those animals higher on the food chain. Current research, as documented in John Robbins' book Diet for a New America, finds that 90% of these contaminants and toxic residues in the average diet are found in meat, dairy products, chicken, eggs and fish. This is in contrast to only 10% in total, from seeds, grains, lentils, legumes, vegetables and fruits. Many consumers have apparently been misinformed in this area and consequently have limited the amounts of fresh produce that they consume for fear of these toxic residues. For those who may be confused with these statistics, just review the feed conversion ratios mentioned earlier in this text (page 13) and they will begin to make more sense to you.

On the more positive side, flesh foods are very concentrated sources of such important nutrients as iron, zinc, vitamin B12 and the essential amino acids (proteins). As such, they can fill important gaps in the diets of those who, for whatever reason, do not eat a complete diet or do not digest a more plant-based diet very well. In order to facilitate their digestion, flesh foods are best eaten with the high water content vegetables. (see Appendix A) This helps to compensate for the lack of fiber in flesh foods and their higher cholesterol content. These vegetables are rich in natural substances called phytosterols which inhibit the absorption of some of the cholesterol consumed at the same meal.

In summary, I advise the reader to hold off the introduction of flesh food until after your infant's first birthday (if you choose to do so at all). -- Use discretion with respect to the sources of your flesh foods; organically-fed and hormone-free being preferred. -- Limit your infant's consumption of flesh foods to several meals weekly and eat them with the high water content vegetables. Carefully observe for any changes in your infant's bowel function. Sour, rancid or foul odour is proof positive that your infant is not digesting these foods properly. Consider once again that flesh foods have no fiber, they contain cholesterol and saturated fat and they are relatively high in undesirable bacteria and waste products such as urea and lactic acid.

Another issue to consider here is that, as stated earlier, the excessive heating or cooking of flesh foods and dairy products has been implicated in the onset of many of the degenerative diseases which now plague our society, yet current (and often less humane*1) animal husbandry practices have resulted in a greatly increased risk to infection from these foods! My advice is that if you can get fresh, organically raised flesh and dairy products locally, don't spoil their nutritional value with excessive heat and cooking. If these are not available to you or you don't feel they are worth the effort to obtain, you are probably best to simply leave them out of your family's diet all together.

Let there be no confusion here for parents who for moral, ethical, ecological, conscientious or specific health reasons, prefer not to feed their infant any flesh food; you can still meet their nutrition needs amply in the majority of cases. This simply necessitates the regular inclusion of lentils, legumes, grains, seeds and nuts to meet similar protein and mineral requirements. As for concerns about vitamin B12 deficiency from a meatless diet, I have yet to see a patient (infant or adult) who is deficient in this important nutrient, vegetarian or not, unless they have had either a malabsorption problem or an imbalance in their intestinal bacteria. These situations can be monitored and rectified if need be, under the direction and supervision of your health coach.

---

*1   The less humane husbandry practices to which I refer are: the overcrowding, the force feeding, the lack of exercise, the lack of natural light, the separation of the young from their mothers and the lack of love and respect from their handlers.

An Overview

The following timeline is presented for your reference only. The specifics of your situation may very well dictate a different schedule for you and your infant. Those specifics will be up to you and your health coach to determine, cooperatively.

Birth to 6 months of age   •Breast-feeding

6 - 9 months   •Breast-feeding, fresh fruits, vegetables, seed and nut milks.*

9 - 12 months   •Breast-feeding, fresh fruits, vegetables, seed, nut and soy milks, lentils.*

12-18 months   •Breast-feeding (optional, but beneficial yet), fresh fruits, vegetables, seed, nut and soy milks, lentils, legumes, non-gluten grains, live-culture yogurt and raw certified milk (optional).*

18-24 months   • Breast-feeding (optional, but still beneficial, fresh fruits, vegetables, seed, nut and soy milks, lentils, legumes, non-gluten grains, gluten grains, and in those cases where these are tolerated well 'healthy' flesh foods and 'healthy' dairy products.*

24 months on • Follow the guidelines found in
Functional Dietetics, The Core of
Health Integration and Guilt-free
Indulgence, An Art Worth Mastering.

*With the addition of the essential oils, beneficial bacteria, food concentrates and multiple vitamin/mineral preparations as prescribed by your health coach.

A Final Note to Parents and Guardians,

May I express my respect and sincere appreciation for your time and dedication in reviewing this material. It has been written in order to share the information and experiences with you, which I and many others, have found significant in the area of infant nutrition and health. The concepts have been written in a comprehensive fashion so as to provide you, the person *responsible* for your infant's health, with a set of *guidelines*, from which you may proceed with the support of your health coach in safeguarding your infant's health.

I trust that you have found this information valuable and that it will contribute significantly to your understanding of the complex and challenging task of determining which foods are best suited for your infant.

I acknowledge that even in the best of scenarios, attending to an infant's needs is a full-time plus responsibility. In the 'less than desirable' scenarios, attempts to meet an infant's needs can demand more of the parents than they feel they have to give. No matter what challenges you face in attending to your infant's needs, please do not limit yourself with self-defeating dialogue like, "It's probably just a phase that my child is going through, so we will just have to try to hang on and wait until they grow out of it". A distressed infant *never* grows out of *it* or anything else. After so many weeks, months or even years, the infant's or then child's system simply quits displaying the distress in the same fashion, the symptoms are suppressed and the distress and resultant dysfunction continues only more covertly. Such covert dysfunction often leads to the eventual onset of one of the degenerative diseases with so called 'unknown causes' later in life. Please listen to your instincts, you know when your infant is in distress so work with your health coach to find and alleviate its cause.

I have had the good fortune of working with literally hundreds of irritable, multi-symptomatic infants over the past decade. Every one of these infants has responded positively to a cooperative strategy between parents, guardians and health coach, aimed at eliminating step by step the possible irritants and unnecessary stressors in their environment. This, in many cases, has not been easy and indeed has required a good deal of patience, concentration and careful observation by all parties involved. The demand can appear great during this process of identifying cause and effect. Yet in comparison to the ongoing heart-wrenching and nerve-racking experience of helplessly witnessing your infant suffer, it is really quite acceptable and straightforward, with patience and discipline being the most important prerequisites.

For those who are inclined to think that all of this is too much bother and who consider drugs to be an acceptable response to your infant's health and behaviour challenges, I urge you to refer to your P.E.P. binder or ask your participating Health Coach® for the article entitled "Understanding the Action of Drugs, in Relation to Natural Laws." Your health coach, is likely to have a variety of non-toxic, non-invasive therapeutic approaches, in addition to the dietetics discussed in this book, which will serve to facilitate your infant's recovery. The therapies which they use promote the same vital force which has guided your infant's magical development from the union of a single sperm and egg cell to the incredible little being that they are now. Please respect the wisdom and the power of the life force which made them by choosing therapies which work with it, not against it. Suppressing Mother Nature with powerful, often toxic allopathic drugs should only be considered in the most severe and threatening of cases.

Your health coach, if they are a licensed primary contact health professional should be trained to differentiate the nature and severity of your child's condition and to either administer the indicated therapy or to refer you to the appropriate specialist. If you have any questions about their training or competence in this area of differential diagnosis, be certain to get second opinions with any significant health challenges. You do usually have more options than just drugs and surgery available to you, so be sure to explore and utilize them where appropriate.

As for any arguments like "Mom and Dad never raised me on this type of diet and I feel fine, so why bother with all of the fuss?", I have little doubt that the vast majority of Moms and Dads have done the very best they knew how to raise and feed their infants properly. They however were not likely to have access to the kind of information within this book in the past, and even if they did, statistics in those days had no way of revealing the vast current of degeneration which would besiege their children and subsequent generations. In the past six decades, soaring rates of such degenerative diseases as: heart disease, osteoporosis, arthritis and many forms of cancer have led health scientists and practitioners alike to take a much closer and more candid look at the role which nutrition has been playing. As a result, there has been an about-face in the healthcare community and the field of nutrition has a new found emphasis in the areas of disease prevention and health promotion. In the light of statistics which suggest that fifty percent of parents today will die of some form of heart or circulatory disease and one third of all parents today will develop some form of cancer, perhaps the subjective comment of: "I'm doing fine..." should not be given too much weight here.

As with all lifestyle choices, you are ultimately the judge. I would have it no other way. I simply seek to inform you, the reader, of additional options. It has been my experience that often parents feel that they have exhausted all options, when indeed they have only exhausted the few options which they were aware that they had. Understanding that our *focus* becomes our *reality*, it would appear to be in our best interest to broaden our focus whenever the opportunity presents itself.

Certainly, the approach to infant nutrition, outlined in this book, is more involved than opening a can of infant formula or a jar of pablum, but where in life have you truly benefited without significant involvement on your part? How important is your infant's current and future health to you?

In closing, I would like to leave you with two quotes that continue to influence the choices which I make in my life, day in and day out. The first is...

"If you do not make time for health, you will eventually have to make time for disease."

Which would you prefer to make time for? If you are unsure of your answer here, I encourage you to ask someone who is currently ill this same question.

The second quote is:

"Discipline weighs ounces, in comparison to regret which weighs pounds."

May you and your loved ones make time to attend to your nutrition and health needs and have no future regrets.

With love and respect for all life,

Mark Percival D.C., N.D.

Founder, Health Coach Systems International

APPENDICES

APPENDICES

How to get the most from what you eat!

To clarify an old adage, we are not what we eat, but we are what we properly digest and absorb; physiologically speaking of course! How we eat our foods is as important as what we eat. In order to assure that you and yours receive the maximum benefit from what you eat, please consider the following points carefully.

- **Make the time to relax** before you eat or drink. We do not digest properly when we are anxious. The dinner table is no place for 'heated' debates.

- **Always give thanks** for what you have and for what you are about to receive. Sixty-three million people will die of starvation in our world this year. Every two seconds, a child dies of starvation, somewhere in our world. Whatever you or your infant are about to eat, appreciate the opportunity.

- **Drink the majority of your fluids between and before meals.** This minimizes the dilution of important digestive enzymes, when you need them the most.

- **Chew all food to liquid** and sip all liquid foods slowly, being sure to mix them well with saliva, in order to ensure this essential first stage of digestion.

- **Review the principles of 'food combining'** as different foods require different digestive processing, and enzymes, for their proper digestion and absorption. The chart found on the following page will provide you with an overview, however for specific information refer to <u>Functional Dietetics</u>, section on Proper Digestion and Assimilation pages 69 to 83. This is especially important for those with any digestive or gastrointestinal challenges (infants included).

- **Refrain from overeating.** Due consideration of the above points and their effective practice will assist you here. Simply be conscious of how you feel before, during and after all meals. This will help you to know when you have met your real needs. Try to eat so as to feel at least as well after you eat, as you did before. That's right, you don't have to feel bloated or lethargic after meals! Nor does your infant need a bottle everytime he or she gets restless.

- **Refrain from the ritual of dessert.** If you choose to eat dessert foods, do not let them spoil the proper processing of your lunch or dinner; eat them some hour or more later on and try to spare your child from the 'dessert habit'.

- **Tune in, and learn to listen to your body.** Eating should not be stressful or create any discomfort. If you are practising the above principles and you or your infant are still experiencing any discomfort around eating or di gestion, be sure to discuss this with your health coach.

Simplifying Digestion Through Better Food Combining

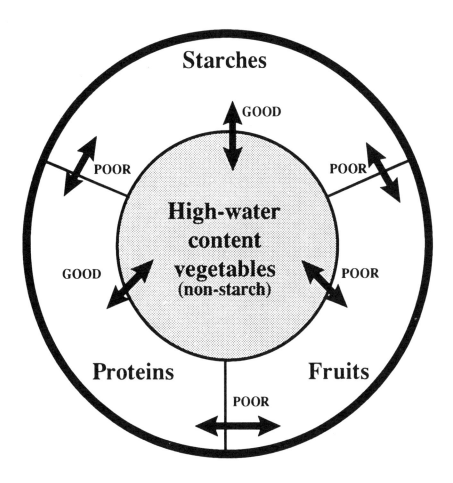

GOOD = Presents little digestive challenges for most
POOR = Presents considerable digestive challenges for some

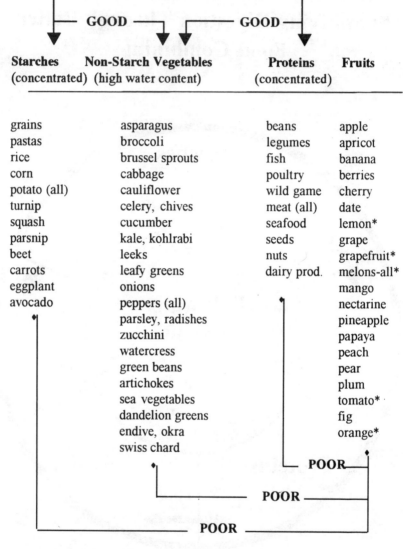

Starches (concentrated)	Non-Starch Vegetables (high water content)	Proteins (concentrated)	Fruits
grains	asparagus	beans	apple
pastas	broccoli	legumes	apricot
rice	brussel sprouts	fish	banana
corn	cabbage	poultry	berries
potato (all)	cauliflower	wild game	cherry
turnip	celery, chives	meat (all)	date
squash	cucumber	seafood	lemon*
parsnip	kale, kohlrabi	seeds	grape
beet	leeks	nuts	grapefruit*
carrots	leafy greens	dairy prod.	melons-all*
eggplant	onions		mango
avocado	peppers (all)		nectarine
	parsley, radishes		pineapple
	zucchini		papaya
	watercress		peach
	green beans		pear
	artichokes		plum
	sea vegetables		tomato*
	dandelion greens		fig
	endive, okra		orange*
	swiss chard		

POOR — GOOD — GOOD — POOR — POOR — POOR

* Citrus fruits and melons often do not mix well with other fruits. May be best eaten alone.

Note: The recipes in the book <u>Guilt-Free Indulgence - An Art Worth Mastering</u>, have taken the principles of food combining into consideration and should not place undue stress on your digestive system.

Low Lactose, Low Fat Yoghurt

- Bring one quart (or litre) of skim milk to the simmer stage and remove from the heat. Stir often to prevent scorching and sticking to the bottom of the pan.

- Cover and cool until it has reached room temperature or below (may be placed in the refrigerator to hasten cool ing). It is important that you allow the temperature to drop sufficiently (to below 120° F / 48° C) or you may kill the bacterial culture you are now ready to introduce.

- Remove 1/2 cup of cooled milk and mix (make a paste) with 1 level tablespoon of Ultra Dopholius or Ultra Bifidus (2 uniquely beneficial strains of 'healthy' bacteria) or 2 teaspoons of each.

- Mix the paste with the remainder of the cooled milk and stir thoroughly.

- Pour the milk into a container, cover and let stand *for at least 24 hours.* The fermentation should not be less than 24 hours. If you forget to remove it after 24 hours, all the better. The source of heat during the 24 hour fermenta- tion is critical. It is important to get the temperature between 100 - 110°F (38 - 43 C.) before you proceed with the fermentation. Too high of a temperature will kill the bacterial culture and will prevent the proper conversion of the lactose. Too low a temperature will prevent the activation of bacterial enzymes and will result in incom- plete digestion of lactose. An electric yoghurt maker controls the temperature perfectly but the amount you can make at one time is limited. A temperature-regulating electric warming tray is the ideal source of heat. Use a mouth thermometer to set the dial properly. An electric crock pot (set low) or a heating pad may be used. If you have a gas oven, the pilot light usually keeps the temperature within the correct range. Turning the oven light on (with a 60 watt bulb) should create enough warmth to make the yoghurt. Upon completion of yoghurt fermentation, replace with a regular oven light bulb.

- Allow the yoghurt to remain on the heat for at least 24 hours to insure that all lactose is completely digested. Remove from the heat and refrigerate. This yoghurt may not be as thick as commercial yoghurt but virtually all the lactose has been digested by the bacterial culture and there is no further digestion required by the intestinal cells, and therefore little chance of any intolerance or ill effects.

Grain Preparation Chart

Grain (1 cup dry measure)	Water	Cooking Time	Yield
Amaranth*	2 cups	20 minutes	1-1/2 c
Barley (whole)	3 cups	1 hour 15 min.	3-1/2 c
Brown rice ** (short/long grain)	2 cups	45 minutes	3 cups
Buckwheat (kasha)**	2 cups	15 minutes	2-1/2 c
Bulgur wheat	2 cups	15-20 minutes	2-1/2 c
Coarse cornmeal ** (polenta)	4 cups	25 minutes	3 cups
Cracked wheat	2 cups	25 minutes	2-1/3 c
Millet**	3 cups	30-45 minutes	3-1/2 c
Oats	1-1/2 cups	30 minutes	2-1/2 c
Quinoa*	2 cups	15 minutes	3 cups
Rye	3 cups	1 hour	2-1/2 c
Spelt	1-1/2 cups	30 minutes	2-1/2 c
Triticale	3 cups	30-60 minutes	2-2/3 c
Wild rice**	2 cups	1 hour or more	3 cups
Whole wheat berries	3 cups	2 hours	2-2/3 c

* denotes very low gluten content
** denotes gluten-free grains.

Note: If grains are presoaked overnight, drain the soaking water, decrease cooking water by 1/2 cup and decrease cooking time by approximately 10 minutes.

Sprouting Grains: The kernels or seeds of grains are like nuggets of energy and nutrients. Sprouting them unlocks and amplifies their natural sweetness and nutritional profile. All you will need is a small bowl, pure water and 1/3 to 1/2 cup unhulled kernels (rye, soft and hard wheat, barley, buckwheat and triticale are the grains of choice here). Cover the grains with pure water for 24 hours, cover with a lid and let sit on the counter overnight. Drain the grains (reserve the vitamin-rich water and use it for cooking) and allow them to sit, covered, for approximately 12 hours or until sprouted. They are then ready to be enjoyed. No cooking or heating is necessary. Simply puree these well and add to your infant's vegetable, legume, grain, seed or nut servings.

Legume Preparation Chart

Bean (1 cup dry measure)	Water	Cooking Time	Yield
Black beans	4 cups	1-1/2 hours	2 cups
Black-eyed peas	3 cups	1 hour	2 cups
Garbanzos (chickpeas)	4 cups	3 hours	2 cups
Great northern beans	3-1/2 cups	2 hours	2 cups
Kidney beans	3 cups	1-1/2 hours	2 cups
Lentils and split peas	3 cups	45 minutes	2-1/4 c
Limas	2 cups	1-1/2 hours	1-1/4 c
Baby limas	2 cups	1-1/2 hours	1-3/4 c
Pinto beans	3 cups	2-1/2 hours	2 cups
Red beans	3 cups	3 hours	2 cups
Small white beans (navy, etc.)	3 cups	2-1/2 hours	2 cups
Soybeans	4 cups	3 hours or more	2 cups
Soy grits	2 cups	15 minutes	2 cups

Preparing and cooking suggestions:

First, rinse the legumes thoroughly and remove any tiny stones or discoloured legumes. Two methods of preparation are described below:

1. Place the rinsed legumes in a pot, add enough pure water to cover them by several inches and boil for 15 minutes. Turn off the heat and let sit for at least 2 hours. Drain off the water, add new pure water and simmer for 30-45 minutes or until tender.

2. Soak the dried legumes in pure water for 24 hours on the counter or for 48 hours in the fridge. Dried legumes will double or triple in volume when cooking is complete, so be certain that you always keep them well covered with water. Drain the soaking water to cut down on any gas formation problems, and place them in a pot of fresh water. Bring them to a boil, turn down the heat and simmer for 25-40 minutes, or until soft. A good rule of thumb is to cook the legumes until they are 'crushable' when placed between your tongue and the roof of your mouth. Puree and serve. Reserve the legume stock for making great soups.

Note: Lentils and legumes are best eaten alone, by themselves, in order to assist their proper digestion. If your infant experiences excessive gas or bloating after legumes, be sure to ask your Health Coach about supplementary digestive enzymes.

The Diversified Rotation Diet

Another step in the development of more supportive eating habits is to master the rotation of your foods and food families.

Rotating your diet and that of your infant has a number of distinct advantages:

1) It ensures a wider variety of foods in your diet, helping to ensure more complete nutrition.

2) It minimizes exposure to potential food allergens and/or residual contaminants and toxins which may be present in a particular food family. Thereby enhancing the body's ability to deal more effectively with these potential food stressors.

3) It facilitates the identification of any undesirable foods in your diet, by allowing you to observe any signs or symptoms which may follow the ingestion of a specific food.

By rotating your diet, your body does not have to struggle with any repetitive food stressors with the same frequency that it has in the past. As your body becomes healthier and less stressed, it will let you know which foods to avoid with more clarity. Now be sure to listen to it!

The exception to the principle of rotating foods and their families for better health occurs when you have access to fresh organically and regionally grown foods. This of course would support more frequent seasonal consumption of these foods. The availability of quality foods also influences one's ability to rotate their diet 'ideally'. The reader is encouraged to take all factors into consideration and to do their best accordingly. Where any confusion exists, simply consult your health coach.

What does *diversified* mean? Not only are you going to rotate different foods, but you will also rotate different *food families*. Certain foods are so similar botanically that sensitivities to one food can create sensitivities to another. For instance, if you are allergic/sensitive to oranges, you may also be allergic/sensitive to grapefruit. So which foods are in which *family?*

1) ALGAE
Agar
Dulse
Kelp

2) APPLE
Apple
Pear
Quince

3) BANANA
Banana
Plantain

4) BIRCH
Filbert
Hazelnut

5) BUCKWHEAT
Buckwheat
Rhubarb

6) CASHEW
Cashew
Mango
Pistachio

7) CITRUS
Mandarine
Grapefruit
Kumquat
Lemon
Lime
Orange
Tangerine

8) COMPOSITE
Artichoke
Camomile
Chicory
Dandelion
Endive
Escarole
Head Lettuce
Leaf Lettuce
Safflower
Tarragon

9) FUNGUS
Cheese (all)
Mushrooms
Sour Dough
Vinegars
All Yeasts

10) GINGER
Cardamom
Ginger
Tumeric

11) GOOSEBERRY
Currant
Gooseberry

12) GOOSEFOOT
Beets and
Beet sugar
Lamb's quarter
Swiss chard
Spinach

13) GOURD
Cantaloupe
Casaba
Cucumber
Honeydew
Melons (all)
Pumpkin and seeds
Squash (all)
Veg. Marrow
Watermelon
Zucchini

14a) CEREAL
Barley
Bulgur
Gluten
Malt
Rye
Triticale
Wheat
Bran
Wheat Germ
Graham

14b) CEREAL
Oats

14c) CEREAL
Corn
Millet

14d) CEREAL
Rice
Wild Rice

14e) CEREAL
Bamboo Shoot
Sugar Cane
Molasses
Sorghum

15) GRAPE
Cream of Tartar
Grape
Raisin

16) HEATH
Blueberry
Cranberry

17) LAUREL
Avocado
Bay Leaves
Cinnamon

18) LEGUMES
Alfalfa Beans &
Sprouts
Carob
Chick Pea
Snow Pea
Kidney Bean
Lecithin
Lentils
Licorice
Lima Bean
Mung Bean
Navy Bean
Split Pea
Peanuts & Butter
Pinto Bean

All Dried Peas
Soy Bean
Tofu
String Bean
Tamarind

19) LILY
Asparagus
Chive
Garlic
Leek
Onion
Shallot

20) MALLOW
Okra
Cottonseed

21) MAPLE
Syrup
Sugar

22) MINT
Basil
Marjoram
Mint
Oregano
Peppermint
Sage
Savory
Spearmint
Thyme

23) MULBERRY
Fig
Hop
Mulberry

24) MUSTARD
Bok Choy
Broccoli
Brussel Sprouts
Cabbage
Cauliflower
Collard
Horseradish
Kale
Kohlrabi
Mustard
Radish
Rapeseed
Rutabaga
Turnip
Watercress

25) MYRTLE
Allspice
Clover
Cloves
Guava

26) NUTMEG
Mace
Nutmeg

27) OLIVE
Black
Green
Olive Oil

28) PALM
Coconut
Date

29) PARSLEY
Anise
Caraway
Carrot
Celery
Coriander
Cumin
Dill
Fennel
Parsley
Parsnip

30) PLUM
Almond
Apricot
Cherry
Nectarine
Peach
Plum
Prune

31) POTATO
Cayenne
Chili Pepper
Eggplant
Green Pepper
Paprika
Pimento
Potato
Red Pepper
Tobacco
Tomato

32) SPURGE
Cassava
Tapioca

33) ROSE
Blackberry
Raspberry
Strawberry
All Berries
Rosehip

34) STERCULA
Cocoa
Cola
Chocolate

35) SUNFLOWER
Jerusalem Artichoke
Sunflower Oil
Sunflower Seeds

36) TEA
Green Tea
Pekoe Tea

37) WALNUT
Butternut
Hickory Nuts
Pecan
Walnuts
Pineapple
Pine Nut
Pomegranate
Poppy Seed
Quinoa
Saffron
Sesame Oil & Seeds
Sweet Potato/Yam
Taro Root
Vanilla

SEAFOOD
A) Crustaceans
Crab
Shrimp
Crayfish
Lobster
Prawn

B) Mollusks
Squid
Abalone
Clam
Mussel
Oyster
Scallop

SALT WATER FISH
C) Anchovy

D) Cod
Haddock
Hake

E) Flounder
Halibut
Sole
Turbot

F) Mackerel
Albacore Tuna

G)Red Snapper

FRESH WATER FISH

H) Herring
Sardine
Shad

I) Pike
Muskie

J) Salmon
Trout

K) Smelt

L) Sturgeon
Caviar

M) Sunfish
Black Bass
Bluegill
Crappy

BIRDS
N) Chicken
Cornish Hen
Duck
Goose
Grouse
Pheasant
Pigeon
Quail
Turkey
All Eggs

MEAT	**R) Porcine**	**T) Rabbit**
O) Bovine	Bacon	
Dairy Products	Ham	**U) Buffalo**
Beef	Pork	
Veal		

P) Goat & Goat Products

Q) Lamb	**S) Moose**
Mutton	Venison

Note: The 'Animal Kingdom' is less clear cut for food family rotation purposes. Be aware that the above groups are academic guides for possible cross reactions, but the most useful guide will be one's own testing and experience.

Your goal here should be to eat from a specific food family approximately once every four days. A simple menu plan actually makes this challenge quite simple.

In most instances this does require a considerable shift from prior eating habits, as most eat a surprisingly monotonous diet with respect to the actual ingredients of their foodstuffs. The most important foods to rotate are: those higher on the food chain and thus more likely to have accumulated various chemical residues (ie. flesh foods), those foods that you should not eat frequently anyway due to their high saturated fat or low fibre content, those foods that you suspect you or someone in your family may be allergic to, or intolerant of.

Those who make the effort here, find it to be a uniquely rewarding endeavour. After all, is 'variety' not one of life's key spices?!

THE COACH'S SUPER FORMULA

Dairy-free and suitable for infants and athletes alike as a high-energy, nutrient-rich beverage.

Ingredients:

5 cups pure water (rice included) or 3 cups water
    (rice excluded)
1 cup cooked whole grain rice (optional*)
3 tbsp. raisins
2 tbsp. almonds (freshly ground)
2 tbsp. raw grated beets (1 small)
2 tbsp. grated carrots (1 small)
2 tbsp. sunflower or pumpkin seed (freshly ground)
2 tbsp. sesame seeds (freshly ground)
1 tbsp. flax oil
1/2 tsp. buffered Vitamin C powder
1 scoop Health Gain metabolic optimizer (available
through your participating Health Coach® center)
Honey or unsulphured blackstrap molasses to taste
    (optional)

*Due to its relatively high starch content, *some* infants below the age of 1 may not digest even rice very well. If this is the case with your infant, just omit step 1 and simply add the raisins only in step 2. You may wish to soak or simmer them first however to soften and facilitate blending.

As with any combination of foods, be sure to first introduce all ingredients singularly observing closely for any ingredients which don't agree with your infant and then just leave these out.

Preparation:

- Add 1/2 cup of uncooked rice and 3 tablespoons raisins to 1-1/3 cups water and simmer for 45 minutes.
- Place the cooked rice and raisin mixture in a blender or Vita-Mix, with 1 cup water, and blend to liquid.
- Add the fresh raw grated carrots and beets, and liquefy.
- Add ground almonds, seeds, flax oil, buffered C powder and Health Gain, and blend once again, adding the remaining 2-2/3 cups of water slowly.
- If more sweetness is desired by your infant or an adult, add molasses or honey to taste. For very young infants or bottle-feedings, strain the mixture through a fine mesh strainer or a cheese cloth to remove any solids. Keep these nutritious solids for use later in porridges, cereals and/or baking.

The following recipes are a few flavour enhancers which may be added to your infant's purees of vegetables, legumes or grains, etc to enhance their appeal. As your infant gets older and able to chew properly, you will find their use as sauces helpful in encouraging your child to eat more whole, healthy foods. Bon Appetit!

RAISIN SAUCE

For something a little sweeter and a delight for most children this is a great sauce over grains and vegetables (once they have been properly introduced, of course).

Ingredients:

2 tbsp. safflower oil
3 tbsp. whole wheat or oat flour *
1 cup fresh apple juice
1 cup chopped raisins or whole currants
1/8 tsp. sea salt (optional)

Preparation:

- <u>Gently</u> heat the oil in a saucepan, then add flour and stir constantly for a minute.
- Slowly add the apple juice, taking care lumps do not form.
- Cook slowly, stirring frequently until the sauce has thickened.
- Add raisins and simmer gently for 4 minutes, stirring regularly to prevent sticking.

Makes 1 cup.

* Where gluten intolerance is suspected, just substitute rice, potato, arrowroot or bean flour here.

SESAME SAUCE

This sauce is delicious over steamed cauliflower, asparagus, potatoes, broccoli or any other vegetables, as well as grains.

Ingredients:

1 tsp. arrowroot powder, dissolved in a little pure water
1 cup pure water
1 tbsp. miso (soya paste)
1 tsp. tahini (sesame paste)
1 tsp. ginger, freshly grated or powdered

Preparation:

- Add the arrowroot powder (already dissolved) to the cup of water in the saucepan.
- Bring to a boil and then simmer for a few minutes until the sauce has thickened.
- Mix in the remaining ingredients and simmer for a few minutes more.

Makes 1 cup of sauce.

HERB SAUCE

An extremely simple sauce to prepare, which can be used over or in almost anything.

Ingredients:

1/2 cup fresh spinach, steamed and squeezed dry
1/2 cup vegetable stock* or use the water after
    steaming vegetables
4 tbsp. flax seed oil
1/2 tsp. dried tarragon
1/2 tsp. dried chervil
1/2 tsp. dried parsley
1/2 tsp. dried thyme
2 tbsp. fresh lemon juice

Preparation:

- Blend all ingredients in a food processor until smooth.
- Add more vegetable stock to thin the sauce if necessary.
- Store in an opaque container, in the refrigerator to protect the essential nutrients.

Makes 4 servings.

* See page 99 of our cookbook <u>Guilt-free Indulgence</u> for details on how to prepare your own vegetable stock for a variety of uses.

ALMOND SPREAD   *(Infant Version)*

Mix this delicious and nutritious spread into any of your infant's foods (except fruit) to give them more flavour and appeal. Although garlic is an exceptionally healthy herb to include in one's diet, it may upset some infants' tummies, so go lightly at first and observe for their tolerance here.

Ingredients:

1/2 cup raw almonds
1/2 to 3/4 cup pure water or soy milk
2 generous tsp. soy powder (optional)
1/2 tsp. salt-free seasoning or seasoned salt
Flax seed oil and sunflower or sesame oil to desired
        consistency (1/2 to 1 cup)
3 tbsp. fresh lemon juice
1/2 tsp. apple cider vinegar (optional) or lemon juice

Preparation:

- Cover almonds with boiling pure water and allow to cool slightly, then remove skins (or simply buy them already blanched)
- Place them in a blender or food processor and grind to a fine powder.
- Add half the water or soymilk, soy powder, and seasoning. Blend well, then add the remaining liquid until a smooth cream is formed.
- With the blender turned on low, drizzle in the oil in a thin stream until the mixture is thickened to desired consistency. Refrigerate in a tightly sealed jar; will keep for 10 days to 2 weeks.
- Store in an opaque container, in the refrigerator to protect the essential nutrients.   Makes 2 cups.

MILD AVOCADO DRESSING

Extremely mild and creamy. Enjoy it over grains or blend it into squash and other starchy vegetables for your infant.

Ingredients:

1 ripe avocado
1/4 cup flax seed oil
1/4 tsp. ground ginger or freshly grated
1 clove garlic, minced (optional)
1 tsp. lemon juice
1 tsp. marjoram

Preparation:

- Toss all ingredients into a blender and process until well blended.
- Intend to use all the dressing, or cut the recipe in half, as the avocado will turn color if it is left too long in the refrigerator.
- Store in an opaque container, in the refrigerator to protect the essential nutrients.

Makes about 1/2 cup.

POPPYSEED DRESSING *(Infant Version)*

An all-time favorite among infants and adults alike.

Ingredients:

2 tbsp. honey
2 tbsp. sesame seeds
1 tbsp. poppy seeds
1/4 tsp. wheat-free Tamari soy sauce
1/4 cup flax seed oil
1/4 cup sunflower or sesame oil
1/4 cup lemon juice

Preparation:

- Simply combine all ingredients in a blender or food processor and process until smooth.
- Store in an opaque container, in the refrigerator to protect the essential nutrients.

Makes about 1 cup.

GINGER DRESSING

Ginger has been used for centuries to enhance digestion and to resolve inflammation. Here is a simple preparation that is both therapeutic and delicious.

Ingredients:

3 tbsp. flax seed oil
1 to 2 tbsp. fresh lemon juice
1 tsp. freshly grated ginger

Preparation:

- Place ingredients in a bowl and whisk together with a fork, or blend a larger quantity of all the ingredients in a blender and retain for future use.
- Store in an opaque container, in the refrigerator to protect the essential nutrients.

Makes about 1/4 cup.

HUMMUS SPREAD OR DIP   *(Infant Version)*

This is a great addition to any grain, legume or vegetable dish and makes a great dip for raw vegetable sticks.

Ingredients:

1-1/2 cups chickpeas
3/4 cup liquid from chick peas or pure water
1/4 cup tahini (sesame butter or ground sesame seeds)
1/4 cup fresh lemon juice
1/4 cup flax seed oil
1 tbsp. wheat-free tamari soy sauce
2 tsp. cumin (optional)
1 tsp. coriander

Preparation:

- Sort and rinse the chickpeas and bring them to a boil in a pot of pure water.
- Reduce heat and simmer for 2 hours, stirring occasionally and adding more water as required.
- When peas are tender, then drain and place in the blender with 3/4 cup liquid.
- Process with tamari and spices until smooth, scraping down the sides a few times. Add juice, oil and tahini, and process until thoroughly blended.
- Refrigerate and serve when required. Hummus can be thin or thick depending on what you may be using it for. It will thicken when it is chilled.

Makes 4 cups.

For more delicious recipes and food preparation suggestions, refer to the guide <u>Guilt-free Indulgence, An Art Worth Mastering</u>. Just use common sense when making any of the recipes, minimizing the garlic, onion or strong spice content of the recipes for your infant, until certain of their tolerance.

Please note that all of the aforementioned sauces, dressings and spreads are cholesterol-free and rich in valuable essential oils, vitamins, minerals and enzymes *when prepared as directed.* **Highest quality oils (as explained in <u>Functional Dietetics</u>, section 'Fats and Oils') are a must here. Be certain that you clarify any confusion here with your Health Coach.** If your local food stores do not carry oils which meet the outlined criteria, your Health Coach should have them available. Oils are very concentrated foods and a little goes a long way, so please do not overdo them in your infant's foods. Signs of excess oil consumption include: loose, greasy stools and oily skin. Your Health Coach will help to determine the right amounts for your infant here.

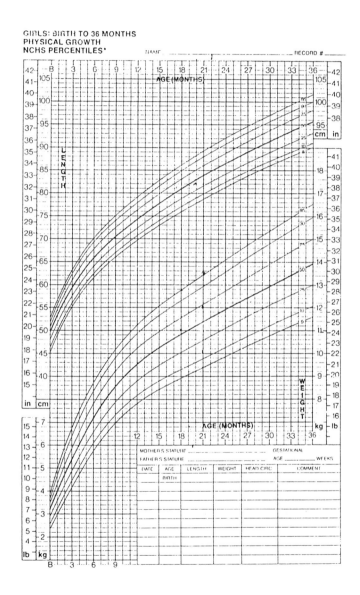

GIRLS: BIRTH TO 36 MONTHS
PHYSICAL GROWTH
NCHS PERCENTILES*

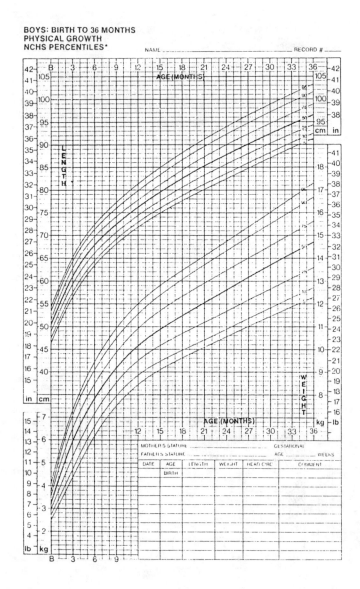

BOYS: BIRTH TO 36 MONTHS
PHYSICAL GROWTH
NCHS PERCENTILES*

NAME _____ RECORD # _____

The following publications and tapes have been authored by Dr. Mark Percival, D.C., N.D., renowned author, lecturer and clinician in the field of nutrition and human behavior. Each work is unique with respect to its content and its pertinence to health. Each is packed with straight-forward information, from both the cutting edge of today's healthcare research and from the wisdom which has resulted from the hundreds of years of recorded experience between humankind and nature. This allows for a unique and highly effective merging of modern science with more traditional medical approaches which have withstood the test of time, yet are now too frequently overlooked. These concepts include such areas as detoxification and traditional foods as our best medicine.

Books:
Guilt-Free Indulgence, An Art Worth Mastering
Functional Dietetics, The Core of Health Integration
Infant Nutrition, Your Child's Foundation for Health
Teaming Up For A Healthier You,
    Understanding Healthcare and Stress Mgmt.

Video Workshops:
The Disease-Toxicity Connection
The Diet-Health Connection (6 video series)
The Mind-Body Connection (4 video series)

Audio Workshops:
The Disease-Toxicity Connection